MAD MURDERERS

BLITZ EDITIONS

Copyright © Bookmart Ltd 1993

All rights reserved. No part of this publication may be reproduced,
stored in a retrieval system, or transmitted in any form or by any
means, electronic, mechanical, photocopying, recording or otherwise,
without prior written permission from the publishers.

Published by Blitz Editions
an imprint of Bookmart Ltd
Registered Number 2372865
Trading as Bookmart Ltd
Desford Road
Enderby
Leicester LE9 5AD

ISBN 1 85605 138 2

This material has previously appeared in *The Encyclopedia of True Crime*.

Every effort has been made to contact the copyright holders for the pictures.
In some cases they have been untraceable, for which we offer our apologies.
Special thanks to the Hulton-Deutsch Collection, who supplied the majority of pictures,
and thanks also to the following libraries and picture agencies:
Cassidy and Leigh, Popperfotos, Syndication International, Topham

Designed by Cooper Wilson Design

MAD MURDERERS

JOHN DUFFY
The Railway Rapist

John Duffy used railway timetables to plot his escapes from the scenes of his beastly crimes. Finally it was his frightened wife who lead the police to the elusive rapist-killer, the man whose laser beam eyes mesmerised his terrified victims.

Number One Court, Old Bailey, London. Within these walls have stood some of the most wicked men and women in history. The courtroom, its atmosphere heavy with the full majesty of British law, has been silent witness to the infamous, the gruesome, the chilling, the unbelievable and the shameful. In 1988, yet another villainous soul was brought to justice. He stood before Mr Anthony Hooper, prosecuting Queen's Counsel. The accused was a rapist and a murderer called John Duffy. Thanks to Mr Hooper's eloquence and mastery of courtroom drama, Duffy earned the sobriquet 'the Killer with Laser Beam Eyes'.

That was how Mr Hooper, in his opening arguements at the trial of John Duffy, described the former altar boy. Duffy, who was thirty years old at the time of the trial, had been in custody since November 1986, trapped by his own insatiable thirst for rape and murder. He was suspected of at least three gruesome slayings, and the police attributed two more to him. He was the very worst type of sex criminal – insatiable, ruthless, and absolutely without remorse. After he received a sentence of life imprisonment with the recommendation from judge Mr Justice Farquaharson that the prisoner serve a minimum of forty years, the policeman who trapped him, Deputy Superintendent John Hurst of Surrey CID, said: 'He is a cold-blooded, calculating killer with a razor-sharp mind. In my twenty-two years experience battling crime, I have never come across a man so calculating and cunning. He is very intelligent and alert. He gave me the impression of being able to react to any type of situation in which he found himself. He is purely evil.'

But there will never be total satisfaction for Mr Hurst who believes that, on several of the rapes Duffy committed he was with a partner. That partner has never been found and, while police have a strong suspicion as to his identity, he is still out on the streets.

John Duffy used London's railway network to travel in search of his rape victims. One of six children born to Irish Catholic parents in Eire, he came to Britain as a child and worked at various jobs after leaving school. He married, in 1980, a plump, stocky woman called Margaret Mitchell but the marriage was not a happy one. In fact, his violence towards her helped give the police a clue to his identity as a rapist. He lived in a flat with Margaret in Barlow Road, Kilburn, where the wife who had thought he was a kind-natured, quiet fellow, watched him change into a brooding, silent monster. He would look at her with those eyes... the eyes that burned

HIS WIFE WATCHED HIM CHANGE INTO A BROODING, SILENT MONSTER. HE WOULD LOOK AT HER WITH THOSE EYES...

Opposite: ***John Duffy whose dislike of women drove him to rape, then murder.***

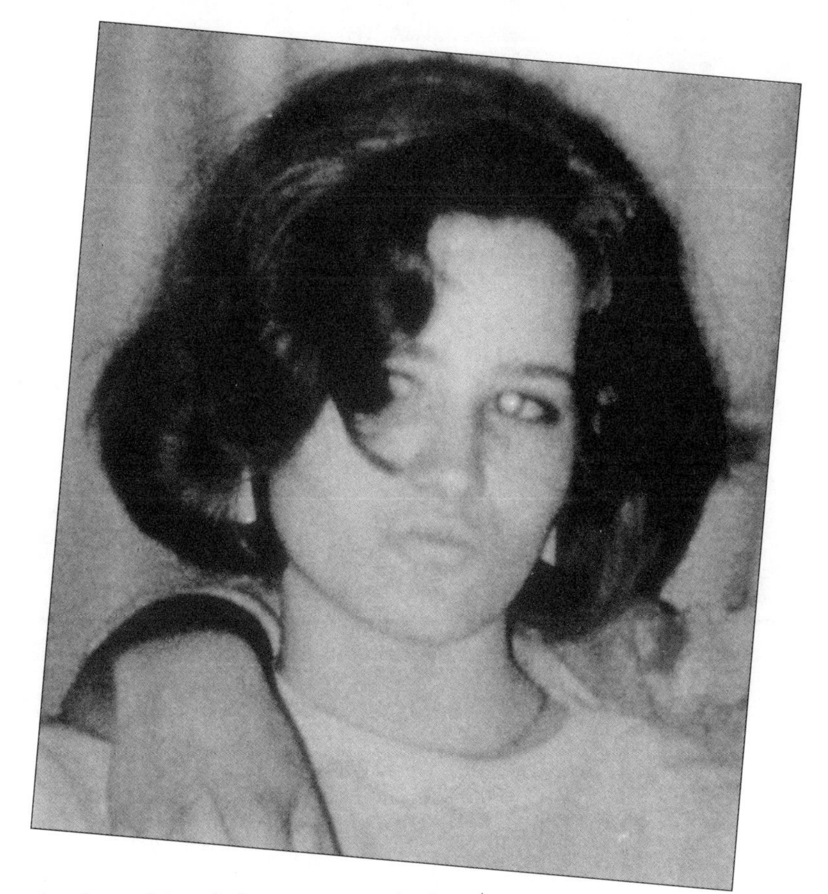

Above: ***Maartje Tamboezer who was only fifteen when Duffy killed her.***

into people, instilling fear. The disillusioned Margaret testified at his trial: 'The nice man I married turned into a raving monster with scary, scary eyes. He taunted me that he liked rape. He said it was the natural thing for a man to do.'

Duffy, sensitive about his small stature (he was only five foot four inches), bolstered his confidence with lessons in karate and the martial arts. At a centre near his home, he spent three nights a week building up his muscles and perfecting his skill at strangle holds. He would spend hours of his spare time poring over books that idealized the Nazis and he paid particular attention when he studied 'The Anarchist's Cookbook', a terrorists' reference book published in the Sixties that taught how to maim and kill. Duffy learnt from this book the importance of planning an escape route from the scene of any crime and because of this lesson, Duffy managed to evade the police, despite his numerous crimes committed over a long period of time.

For the first two years of his marriage Duffy worked as a carpenter for British Rail. He was fascinated by the rail network both in and around London, and plotted rail routes he could use to travel to and escape from the locations of his crimes. His wife said: 'The first couple of years were not too bad but, when we tried to have a child and he found out he had a low sperm count, things changed. He started to have kinky needs in sex. He wanted to tie me up before we made love. He wanted sex every night and we used to fight. I used to lie there and let him get on with it. He used the cord from my dressing gown and only enjoyed it if I kept struggling. If I didn't move or protest, the interest was gone. The more I protested the more he got aroused.' Margaret, who divorced him in 1986, went on: 'Sometimes he got videos out that had blood all over them, all over the cover. He liked those horrific ones, you know, the real nasties.'

Psychiatrists said that Duffy began to hate women, forming in his mind the distorted impression that, somehow, they were to blame for his infertility. It was this hatred that drove him to make violent attacks on women.

'HE STARTED TO HAVE KINKY NEEDS IN SEX. HE WANTED TO TIE ME UP BEFORE WE MADE LOVE. HE WANTED SEX EVERY NIGHT AND WE USED TO FIGHT.'

Below: ***Police interview commuters at train stations during the search for the 'Railway Rapist'.***

Opposite, above: ***Squads of policemen looked for clues in wasteland around rail tracks after Maartje's death.***

Opposite, below: ***An artist's impression of the criminal based on rape victims' descriptions.***

THE RISK OF MEETING
HIS VICTIMS WAS TOO GREAT

Police say his first rape was committed in June, 1982, near Hampstead Heath and that Duffy was with his accomplice. A twenty-three-year-old woman was dragged into a derelict building, then she was bound and gagged. She was the first victim of twenty-seven attacks against women and police have linked these to Duffy, claiming that some of the crimes were carried out with his accomplice, some alone. When police investigated that first rape, they made the observation that her attacker probably escaped using the North London Line rail network. Thereafter, getaways by rail proved to be the attacker's hallmark.

In 1985, Duffy, perhaps no longer stimulated by rape, began to kill his victims. He was at Hendon Magistrates Court awaiting arraignment on a charge of assaulting his wife. While he was there he recognised, although she did not recognise him, a woman whom he had raped a few

HE HAD LEFT AN UNUSUALLY SMALL-SIZE FOOTPRINT NEXT TO THE BODY... AND A LENGTH OF SWEDISH-MADE STRING AT THE SCENE.

months before. He realised then that he could not risk a possible meeting with his victims after his crimes, and understood, in his twisted mind, that all future victims would have to be silenced for ever.

Duffy often posed as a jogger while out looking for a victim. He donned a loose tracksuit and kept in his pocket a butterfly knife with a razor-sharp blade. To this he added his special 'rapist's kit' that would eventually be used as evidence against him. He carried a box of matches, a length of twine or rag and a piece of wood. These were the tools he used in his role as killer.

He constructed a device known as a 'Spanish Windlass' employed by carpenters to hold glued joints together while they set. Duffy planned to use it as a means of murder, as a garrotte around the necks of the women he chose as victims.

When John Duffy committed the first murder, he was already in the police files. The police, during an exercise called Operation Hart, devised a computer list of all the known sex offenders in Britain and Duffy's name appeared here. And indeed, Operation Hart had been set in motion by Duffy when police set out to find the man responsible for the rape on Hampstead Heath, the man whom police had dubbed the 'Railway Rapist'.

Twenty-seven days after his court appearance in Hendon, where he saw one of the girls he had raped, Duffy took a life. On 29 December 29, 1985, he accosted fair-haired Alison Day, nineteen, a girl described at his trial 'as a teenager with a heart of gold'. Alison was travelling on a train between Upminster and Hackney Wick but Duffy forced her off the train at Hackney. Holding a knife against her Duffy, who revelled in using the most foul language on his victims while uttering terrible threats if the girl did comply with his wishes, pushed Alison into a rat-infested garage block, backing on to the filthy waters of the River Lea. There she was raped then garrotted with the Spanish Windlass made from a piece of alderberry wood. Then he attached a weight to her body and dumped it, like garbage into the Lea. She was not found for seventeen days, by which time any evidence of the criminal had decomposed. All police found that could be handed to the forensic laboratories were some clothing fibres from a tracksuit.

Scotland Yard were hesitant to link the crime into Operation Harts being run by

Above: ***The railway path where Maartje was killed.***

Opposite, above: ***Maartje was riding this bicycle when Duffy molested her.***

Opposite, below: ***A detective helps cordon off the area where Maartje met her death.***

Supt. Hurst's team. The body had been found near a railway line but, the men from the Yard pointed out, the Railway Rapist had never killed before. However, both teams began to feel that the Railway Rapist and the killer were the same man when Dutch-born schoolgirl Maartje Tamboezer, fifteen, was killed.

Maartje was the daughter of a wealthy industrialist whose company had posted him to Britain for several years. She enjoyed the English, often remarking to her friends that she found them so friendly. Maartje was cycling down a footpath near the railway line by her home in West Horsley, Surrey, when Duffy pounced. She was dragged into a nearby copse, her hands were bound around her back and she was raped before Duffy used his Spanish windlass to kill her. Then, he set fire to the lower part of her body, hoping to destroy traces of his semen. But, unwittingly, he

left clues; he had broken a bone in her neck with a blow commonly used by martial arts students; he had left an unusually small-size footprint in the soft earth next to the body; and he left a length of Swedish-made string at the scene.

Next came another rape, this time of a fourteen-year-old girl whose life was spared by Duffy. She gave evidence at his trial, and sobbed uncontrollably, as she described the emotions of a girl who is confronted by a monster like Duffy. She said: 'I was at the train station and he had on a tracksuit with the hood pulled up. He put a knife at my throat and dragged me into woods. He said if I struggled or screamed he would slash my throat. He held me with his other arm so I could not move. He put his arm around me to make it look as if we were a couple from behind, but he still held the knife at my neck. I thought I was about to be killed.

'Before raping me he said: "You had better make it good." Afterwards he seemed pleased. But he did not give a damn about me. I was so frightened and in such a state of shock I did not know what was happening. I thought he was going to slash my throat, or something.'

'BEFORE RAPING ME, HE SAID: "YOU HAD BETTER MAKE IT GOOD".'

In May, there was a murder with which Duffy was charged during his trial at the Old Bailey, but on the direction of Justice Farquaharson, he was acquitted of this crime for lack of evidence.

The killing for which he was acquitted was one which attracted a great deal of publicity in Britain. Anne Lock was a vivacious, happy twenty-nine-year-old newly-wed, who worked as a secretary with London Weekend Television. She was murdered just weeks after returning from her honeymoon in the Seychelles in May, 1986. Led down a dark path beside the railway line at Brookmans Park, Hertfordshire, she was bound up, with a stocking pushed into her mouth, the other one wrapped around her throat. Her body was not found until three months after her death, by which time it was badly decomposed.

Six days before the body of Mrs Lock was discovered police interviewed John Duffy. He was one of a group code-named 'Z Men' by police because his blood

Below: ***Detective Chief Superintendent Vincent McFadden led the hunt for the vicious rapist-killer.***

Above: ***A murder investigation demands laborious care in the search for clues. Here, officers check thousands of rail tickets looking for a fingerprint to lead them to the 'Railway Rapist'.***

matched that found on the body of Maartje Tamboezer. In a large scale search detectives from London, Surrey and Hertfordshire had combined to draw up a list of five thousand suspects taken from the Operation Hart master list of sex and assault criminals. The five thousand men were then investigated by a special team, using computers, that cross-referenced names with indexes detailing descriptions, ages and the methods of attack. Professor David Canter, a leading psychologist from the University of Surrey, helped the police build up a psychological profile of their suspect and Canter predicted correctly the area of London where the killer-rapist lived. There was a special emphasis on any links to railway lines. After all the data was fed into the computers, 1,999 men whose profiles fitted all the categories were given a number and were asked to be interviewed by police officers. Duffy's number came out at 1505 and he was duly seen by officers. If he had never beaten his wife, John Duffy would never have been in the computer system.

This is when the supreme skill at deception employed by Duffy came to the fore. He made up a plausible alibi for the night of the Alison Day attack and managed to convince the officers that he was not a permanent acne sufferer. Several of the rape victims had pointed out that their attacker was badly afflicted with the ailment but Duffy explained that he broke out in spots during moments of high stress only. Police were not entirely happy with his answers, but there was no hard evidence to link him with the attacks. And he refused to give a blood sample, saying he wanted to see a lawyer first. As police marked him down as a 'possible' for re-interviewing, Duffy went to a friend with whom he practised karate and paid him to slash him across the chest with a knife. Then Duffy checked himself into a Middlesex mental hospital, claiming he had been mugged and had lost his memory as a result. This was his last desperate ploy as the police net slowly but surely closed in on him.

In October 1986, while the police worked their way through the rest of the suspects on the list, Duffy checked himself out of the mental hospital to follow his dreadful urge for sexual violence. He picked on another fourteen-year-old

DUFFY CHECKED OUT OF THE MENTAL HOSPITAL TO FOLLOW HIS DREADFUL URGE FOR SEXUAL VIOLENCE.

Above: ***Professor David Cantor, of the University of Surrey, was called in by the police to build up a computor-enhanced, psychological profile of the killer.***

schoolgirl. He blindfolded her, tied her against a tree and raped her. The blindfold slipped as Duffy was attacking the girl and he debated whether to kill her but relented and decided she could live.

THE COMPUTER CAME UP WITH A SINGLE NAME

By this time the police computers were taking over from human guesswork. A rape at Copthall Park, North London, the previous year, was found to have striking similarities to the rape-murder of the Dutch teenager Maartje Tamboezer. Details of that attack and everything else about the offenders – blood type, age, height, weight and methods of attack – were fed into the computer and the machine came up with a single name: Duffy. Professor Canter, who pioneered the system known as Pyschological Offender Profiling, or POP, explained: 'I used a computer programme which I had once used to help a biscuit manufacturer research the popularity of new recipes. A criminal leaves evidence of his personality through his actions in relation to a crime. Any person's behaviour exhibits characteristics unique to that person, as well as patterns and consistencies which are typical of the sub-group to which he or she belongs.

HE DEBATED WHETHER TO KILL HER BUT RELENTED AND DECIDED SHE COULD LIVE.

'To take a simple example, crimes typical of people out of work are more likely to be committed during normal working hours than those typical of people who have jobs. We do not infer a meaning from any one particular clue, however, and that is the way we would differ from Sherlock Holmes. We look for a whole system of patterns. For instance, it is remarkably difficult for people to hide and mask certain aspects of their sexual behaviour, which are indicative of the sort of person they are. There are a great variety of rapes. We look at how the attacker approaches the victim, what goes on in the attack and what happens afterwards. From all the factors taken together we build up the whole picture.'

For two weeks, detectives, under the orders of John Hurst, mounted a massive surveillance operation on Duffy. He was followed literally everywhere and was arrested as he went out one night dressed in his jogging suit, complete with his dreadful 'rape kit' in his pocket.

HIS PERVERTED AMBITION WAS TO BE FAMOUS

Under interrogation he was as cold as ice. One lawmen in on the interviews said: 'He would admit to nothing, just stare at you with those eyes that never blinked. They were like big, black whirlpools in which you could see nothing – no soul, no emotions, no feelings. I imagined my own wife and cringed with pity that those poor women saw those evil eyes as their last image on this earth. He would say nothing, but occasionally, when he knew it looked bad for him, he would murmur: "What can they give me then, eh? Thirty years? No problem. I can do thirty. No trouble?"'

A police search of his flat uncovered clothes that he wore in the attack on Maartje. Forensic experts matched fibres on it with the clothes that she wore on the day she died. And they also found a ball of the Swedish string that he had left alongside the girl's body, together with the four–and-a-half size shoes that he had worn for the attack. They, too, matched the undersized footprint at the scene. Other items taken away included gory videos, 'The Anarchist's Cookbook' terror manual, pornographic magazines, knives and an exercise machine that Duffy used to build up his biceps for the terror locks he used on his victims.

Duffy said nothing during his trial, his eyes remaining unblinking at the judge as the appalling litany of crime was read out. In the end he was found Guilty on two rape charges and two murders.

As he stood to be sentenced, on 26 February, 1988, with the recommendation that he serve forty years in jail, he turned and glared at policeman John Hurst. It was the stare that seemed to say: 'Don't worry – forty years? No trouble.'

But Duffy was hurting inside, not for the people he killed, not for the lives he shattered and the families he tore apart with grief; his own ego was shattered because he had not received more sensational press coverage. While on remand in prison, he had boasted to fellow inmates of joining the ranks of the truly notorious such as the Yorkshire Ripper, the Black Panther and Moors Murderer Ian Brady. He was resentful because the trial of Kenneth Erskine, the demented Stockwell Strangler who killed seven elderly people as they slept, started the same day as his, so deflecting some of the spotlight from John Duffy. A detective said after Duffy was sentenced: 'Perhaps that illusion that he is not truly evil – which he is – is the best punishment for him. In Duffy's perverted mind this was when he would join the ranks of the most notorious criminals in Britain. He wanted star status in the gallery of rogues. He was very, very bitter about the Erskine case.'

The hunt had cost £3 million and involved thousands of man hours. But now, at least for the next forty years, women are safe from one of the most infamous rapist-killers of modern times – the Killer with Laser Beam Eyes.

I CRINGED WITH PITY THAT THOSE POOR WOMEN SAW THOSE EVIL EYES AS THEIR LAST IMAGE ON EARTH.

Below: ***John Duffy at the time of his arrest. In court, he was nicknamed 'the killer with laser beam eyes'.***

MARK CHAPMAN

Death of a Dreamer

Mark Chapman was obsessive. His life was dominated by religious fantasies and a wierd idealism. He stalked and shot John Lennon simply because the musician no longer fulfilled his idea of goodness.

Above: ***The respect and admiration that John Lennon inspired is revealed in the mountain of tributes that rose on the pavement outside his home after he was shot.***

Opposite: ***Mark Chapman, the man who killed John Lennon.***

During the Seventies, the famous and adored John Lennon, Beatle, was living almost as a hermit in New York's gracious Dakota apartment building, facing the city's Central Park. Although he liked the freewheeling, exciting, easy-going nature of New York, he was increasingly paranoid about his own privacy and his own security. He had received his first death threat in 1964 when, as one of the four lads in the world's first supergroup, a note had been handed to him at a concert in France informing him that he was to die at 9 o'clock that night. That threatened execution, like several others which followed, failed to materialise. However, he was aware of his vulnerability and preferred to spend his days safe in his queen-sized bed with Yoko Ono and cocooned against the dangerous world and a greedy public outside.

Yet 6,000 miles and four time zones away lived a man whose desire to kill John Lennon had become a consuming, overwhelming passion. Mark Chapman had been an intense fan of Lennon's since the star's days with the Fab Four. Chapman loved the philosophy of the songs, loved the way Lennon became an emissary for peace and love. But somewhere within Chapman the spark of love was extinguished and instead there flickered the flames of jealousy and hatred. In order to understand what turned Mark David Chapman into the future killer of John Lennon, it is crucial to know something of his childhood and his interests.

He was born to David and Diane Chapman in Atlanta, capital of America's Deep South, in October 1955. His father was a middle-management bank employee, a former air-force sergeant, his mother a housewife who assisted in local charity groups. There was nothing in his early life that was not shared by millions of teenagers the world over – the usual highs and lows over love affairs, a little dabbling in pot, a few beers when he was under age. At fourteen, he ran away for a week and at fifteen he was a 'Jesus freak' with long hair, tie-dyed shirts, a large cross hanging around his neck, and a Bible always tucked under one arm. Always highly-strung, impressionable and always intensely eager to prove his worth, he switched from one fad to another – including drugs. He 'tripped' on LSD and liked to drift off to sleep in a bedroom cloudy with the fumes of marijuana smoke.

'THE LORD SPOKE TO ME'

When he was sixteen, he finished with marijuana and claims he had an 'intense religious experience, far greater than anything that I had ever experienced, before, whereby the Lord spoke to me and made me realise that I had to show the good person within.' Chapman became

'THE LORD SPOKE TO ME AND MADE ME REALISE THAT I HAD TO SHOW THE GOOD PERSON WITHIN.'

assistant director of a summer camp for the local YMCA. Tony Adams, his boss at the local branch, recalled: 'He had real leadership qualities. Mark was a very caring person. Hate was not even in his vocabulary. He said he had experimented with drugs when he was younger but he felt that the Lord had touched him and that his life had been turned around. I think his years working summers here really were magical for him.'Perhaps it was his last happy time.

Below: ***With his head hidden, and wearing a bullet-proof vest, Mark Chapman was flanked by lawmen when he appeared in a New York court to answer a charge of murder.***

He was remembered as a 'Pied Piper' among the children, telling them numerous stories and always keeping and holding their attention. But in 1974 he read the book that was to change his life. Someone, it is not known who, gave him 'The Catcher in the Rye' by J.D. Salinger. This novel of disaffected youth, with its central character of Holden Caulfield alone against a cruel and hostile world, touched a deep, raw nerve within Chapman. He identified with Caulfield. His favourite passage from the book, which he kept quoting to anybody who would listen to him, went: 'I keep picturing all these little kids playing some game in this big field of rye. Thousands of little kids, and nobody's around, nobody big, I mean, except me.' The book had become an anthem, a symbol for disillusioned teenagers the world over, but none took it more to heart, or distorted its meaning more, than Mark Chapman.

Around this time there was a second influence in his mixed-up life – rock music. Tod Rundgren, Jimi Hendrix and Bob Dylan were among his favourites. But the Beatles were his all-time top group and his favourite solo singer was John Lennon. It was not just Lennon's music that he adored; he loved his philosophy, his outspokenness on issues like peace and love and fairness. He even played a guitar and tried to imitate him, but he knew he could never attain his 'genius'. Instead, Chapman concentrated on taking a college degree, hopeful that he could get a full-time paid position with the YMCA at the end of the course. In 1975, after taking a college course, he left for Beirut for a short assignment with the youth organization. It was short lived, due to the civil war which started in the Lebanon,

Afterwards he went to Fort Chaffee, Arkansas, a YMCA resettlement camp for Vietnamese refugees. Here he was a resounding success with the Asian immigrants and earned the undying gratitude and praise of the people he worked for. He had also found personal fulfillment with a girl called Jessica Blankenship whom he adored. But she was to claim that soon after he left Fort Chaffee in December 1975, his mood changed. He began to talk with her about death, about how he believed all life was about dying, that the history of man was the history of war. Now in the grip of continual depressions, he began to talk repeatedly about committing suicide.

THE BEATLES WERE HIS ALL-TIME TOP GROUP AND HIS FAVOURITE SOLO SINGER WAS JOHN LENNON.

THE ANGRY AND OVERWEIGHT GUARD

Jessica had persuaded him to enroll in a strict community college to study for a diploma in the humanities. He needed a degree if he was ever to realise his dream of becoming a YMCA director, but he dropped out after just one term. Jessica left him shortly afterwards. He spent the summer of 1976 at a YMCA camp again but quit in the autumn and became a security guard and, a result, an excellent shot with a gun. The security staff for the Atlanta Area Technical School, where he was hoping to be employed, were expected to score at least sixty on a pistol firing test. Chapman scored an amazing eighty-eight. But he was overweight, embarassed by his appearance and, so,growing angrier with the world day by day.

In 1977, after his parent's marriage split up, he flew to Honolulu, Hawaii.. Hiring a car, he drove to a beauty spot overlooking the Pacific, attached a piece of hosepipe to the exhaust and fed it into the car interior. He was rescued by a passer-by who knocked on the window. Chapman had been in the car for fifteen minutes and wondered why he was not dead. A check on the hosepipe outside showed that the heat of the pipe had burned a hole in it. He was angry that his attempt had been thwarted. He went into hospital for a lengthy period of psychiatric counselling. His mother flew to Hawaii to be near him, but even her presence was unable to lift his spirits; he was aggrieved that with a suicide attempt on his record, he would never attain a decent job with the YMCA.

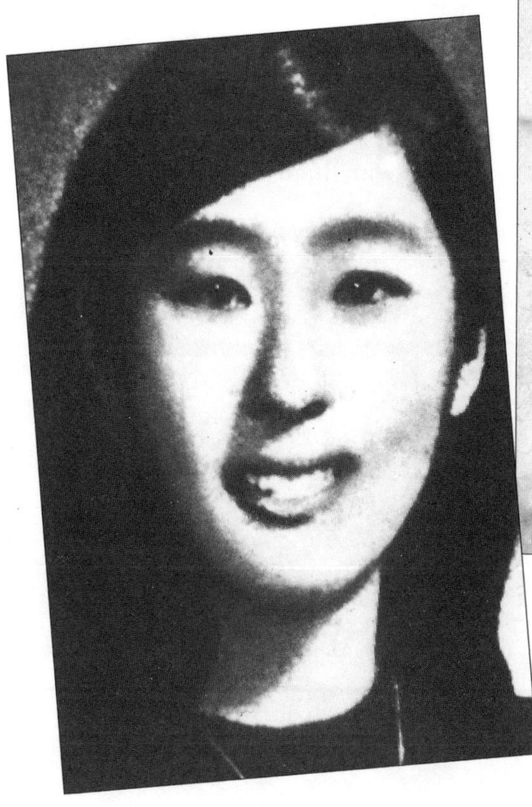

Above, left: ***Gloria Abe Chapman, wife of the deranged killer.***

Above, right: ***The boyish Chapman in a photo taken a few months before he committed his horrible crime.***

In 1978, with money he had saved, combined with a loan from his mother, he took off on a world tour, taking in Tokyo, Seoul, Singapore, Katmandu, Delhi, Israel, Paris and London. On his return to Honolulu, he worked as a hospital housekeeper before striking up a serious relationship with travel agent Gloria Abe, the Japanese-American woman who had sold him his world ticket. His need for companionship and understanding was crucial, even though Gloria's friends found him 'weird and possessive'. He married her in June 1979 – just eighteen months before he would turn to murder.

As the marriage came under increasing strain with ever-more erratic behaviour from Chapman – he spent thousands of dollars he could ill afford on fine works of art – he began to talk darkly of John Lennon's 'sellout'. Gloria heard him fixate on the singer in turgid monologues which blamed his wealth and position for making him 'abandon' his ideals. On 10 September, 1980, Chapman wrote a letter to Lynda Irish, a Honolulu schoolteacher he had befriended. On it he had drawn a picture of the sun, moon and stars above a sketch of an Hawaiian beauty spot. He wrote: 'I'm going nuts.' He signed the letter 'The Catcher in the Rye'. On 23

October, he signed 'John Lennon' on the worksheet at his workplace and four days later purchased a .38 snub nosed revolver.

A few days later, Mark Chapman was in New York, driven by demons whose strength only he fully comprehended. He returned to his birthplace of Atlanta shortly afterwards, telling a local minister that he had been wrestling with the 'good and evil within' but refusing to elaborate. He looked up his old girlfriend Jessica – she would later say that he looked 'disturbed'.

Chapman returned to New York, further depressed when a visit to the YMCA where he had spent happy summers proved to him that he had been virtually forgotten. But his spirits lifted and he telephoned Gloria with news of another religious revelation. 'I've won a great victory,' he said breathlessly. 'I'm coming home. I'll tell you about it when I get there.' But he never arrived – either to see her or keep the appointment he had made several weeks previously with the Makiki Mental Health Clinic.

Chapman began hanging out at the front of the Dakota building, losing himself in the crowd of hangers-on and passers-by who stopped hoping for a glimpse of John Lennon. After Mark's arrest, one man was to claim: 'I saw Chapman on the day of the shooting. I live in that part of town and I remembered also that I had seen him there a couple of days before. You'd always notice people waiting for Lennon. But this guy seemed different. He was shifting back and forth like he was impatient.'

Chapman was staying at the YMCA in the city. He checked out of there on Sunday 7 December and moved into an expensive Sheraton Hotel room nearer to the Dakota. The following day he was back outside, equipped with fourteen hours of Beatles' tape recordings and a copy of the new album by Lennon and Yoko. He also had his gun with him and the ever-present copy of 'The Catcher in the Rye'. In a huddle with other fans, he struck up a conversation with a young blonde fan who was always there. They had lunch together in a restaurant opposite the entrance and returned in the late afternoon, to be joined by another fan called Paul Goresh, an amateur photographer. A few minutes later, at 4.30pm, Lennon stepped outside, accompanied by Yoko. As he walked towards a waiting limousine Chapman stepped forward with a

Above, left: ***John Lennon with his wife, Yoko Ono, in New York two months before his murder.***

Above, right: ***A mother and daughter were among mourners gathered at the death site.***

copy of his Double Fantasy LP in his hand. 'Could I have your autograph, please,' he said almost breathlessly. John paused briefly as Goresh snapped a picture. 'Did I have my hat on or off in the picture?' enquired Chapman. 'I wanted my hat off – they'll never believe this in Hawaii!'

'I JUST SHOT JOHN LENNON'

John Lennon returned again at 11.30pm and Mark Chapman was waiting for him in the shadows. 'Mr Lennon,' he cried out. Then as John turned to see who had spoken, the tormented Chapman assumed the combat stance and killed the musician with five shots. Yoko Ono cradled her husband's head in her arms as the doorman shouted to Chapman: 'Do you know what you just did?' 'I just shot John Lennon,' he calmly replied. Chapman was arrested sitting outside the Dakota building as Lennon was rushed to the Rossevelt Hospital. He was semi-conscious and still-alive, but he had already lost massive amounts of blood. 'It wasn't possible to resuscitate him by any means,' said Dr Stephen Lynn, the hospital's director of emergency services. 'He had lost three to four quarts of blood from the gun wounds, about eighty per cent of his blood volume. The word of his death was broken to Yoko as gently as possible.'

Word spread through the New York night like wildfire. Within one hour one thousand people were outside the Dakota and they stood with candles in a vigil to his memory. The crowd sang Lennon's songs as the tickertapes in countless newspaper offices all over the world clattered out the details of his appalling murder. President Jimmy Carter spoke of the irony that 'Lennon died by violence though he had long campaigned for peace' and President-elect Ronald Reagan called it 'a great tragedy'. The world was saddened.

Chapman was charged with murder and ordered, initially, to undergo thirty days of psychiatric testing. He was first sent, under heavy guard, to a cell at the city's famous Bellvue Hospital where he was placed under a twenty-four-hour suicide watch. But as fears of a revenge killing grew, he was moved to Rikers Island, the city's maximum security jail where his safety could be better guarded. His second attorney – his first quit as the groundswell of public opinion grew more menacing towards Chapman by the day – announced that at his trial the accused would plead Not Guilty by reason of insanity.

When it came to his court hearing in August 1981 Jonathan Marks, his attorney, argued against the prosecution case that Chapman had stalked Lennon before murdering him and had shown no regret. He painted him as a deeply disturbed young man, saying:'All the reports came to the conclusion that he is not a sane man. It was not a sane crime. It was a monstrously irrational killing.' But Chapman himself pleaded Guilty to murder. However, his sanity was definitely in question; whenhe was given time in court to say a few words, he merely quoted a passage from 'The Catcher in the Rye', the book that had become his own gospel.

After he was sentenced to twenty years to life in prison, psychiatrists flocked to America's daytime talk shows to try to explain exactly why Lennon died. Perhaps

'HE STARTED SIGNING HIS NAME AS LENNON. I THINK IT IS SAFE TO ASSUME THAT HE BELIEVED HE WAS JOHN LENNON.'

Below: ***Mark Chapman at Fort Chaffee, Arkansas where he worked in a resettlement camp for Vietnamese refugees. He was well liked by the people in the camp.***

one of the most convincing theories about the motives of Mark Chapman came from Robert Marvit, an Hawaiian psychiatrist. He said: 'He started signing his name as Lennon. I think it is safe to assume that he believed he was John Lennon, or was turning into him. Chapman could have said to himself at the critical point: "My God, Lennon knows there are two of us. I have to reduce it to one." But in the complex package of emotions and hostility which was Mark David Chapman, I am not sure that we shall ever really know what drove him, just what made the ghost in the machine.' But there was no excuse.

'DEMONS' DROVE HIM TO MURDER

It was many years later that the deranged assassin of Lennon spoke for the first time of the 'demons' which drove him to murder – and of how he prays for forgiveness for the awful murder. In 1991 he granted an interview about the events that led up to the shooting, and the killing itself, and he recalled hearing evil whisperings in his head – 'Do it! Do it! Do it!' He claims that he practiced in his hotel room for three days before waiting for Lennon outside his New York apartment building.

'I prayed for demons to enter my body to give me the power to kill,' says Chapman from his cell at Attica Prison in New York State.

Since he was imprisoned, Chapman has received more death threats than any other prisoner in America. Raging Beatle fans have never forgiven him for killing peace-loving Lennon, even his own father cannot forgive him and has never visited him in jail. However, Chapman says he begs forgiveness from God and the world.

Above: ***The murderer as a normal person, playing with a child, before his crazy shooting of John Lennon pushed him to the edge of society and turned him into an outsider.***

Above, top: ***Japanese fans in Tokyo mourn the death of John Lennon.***

He says: 'I became hurt. Enraged at what I perceived to be Lennon's phoniness. I read a photo essay. Put yourself where I was. I saw him on the roof of the luxurious, gabled Dakota building and I showed it to my wife, explaining all about my rage. He told us to imagine. He told us not to be greedy. And I had believed in him! I mean, I had the Beatles pictures on my walls! I believed in those things. They weren't doing them for money. From the time I was ten years old I was listening to all the idealism and truth of John Lennon and I was taking it to heart.

'When it came to the point when my own life was failing I tried to strike it down.' The demented Chapman said he invented 'little people' in his head that he talked with every day, asking them what he should do. It was those 'little people' that who had convinced him he had to murder the famous musician, John Lennon.

'They were appalled,' he said. 'They were shocked. They were still part of my conscience and when I didn't follow my conscience there was no longer any government inside of me. I was on my own. Alone in my apartment, I would strip naked and put on Beatles records and pray to Satan. I prayed for the demons to enter my body to give me the power to kill. I would scream and screech into a tape recorder: "John Lennon must die! John Lennon is a phony!"' The delerious chanting was accompanied by lurid black magic lyrics he taped over John's poignant song 'Strawberry Fields'.

Chapman says he wavered between God and the Devil for two months in 1980 before slipping out to a hardware store where he bought the .38 calibre pistol for £150 and this was the pistol he was to use to shoot John Lennon.

He says he wandered for days 'in a homicidal and suicidal cloud.'

'I prayed, and after struggling back and forth, I won a victory with God's help. I called my wife Gloria and said "your love has saved me. I have won a great victory. I'm coming home." But the demons returned. I went back in December.'

Chapman waited for three days and went to the Dakota building on 8 December with a copy of Lennon's new album 'Double Fantasy'. Chapman said: 'Lennon was very cordial to me. That's something I regret to this day. I handed him the album and he took the black retractable Bic pen and scratched on the album cover to get it going. He stood there trying to get the J going in John and he scratched it a couple of times and laughed. Then he signed 'John Lennon' and wrote 1980 underneath that. Then he handed the album to me and said: "Is this all you want?" His wife was in the car waiting. The door was open. And...I said: "No." I said: "Thanks John." I think of him saying that now: "Is that all you want?" And it seems like, maybe, he had a premonition of his death.

THE DEMONS' ORDERS

'And I was full of wonder that I had a signed album by John Lennon. So much so that I wanted to call the nearest cab and go home to my wife. I wanted to get out of there. But I didn't. I couldn't have gotten out of there. I was totally compelled.'

He returned later that night to complete his berserk quest.

'"Do it! Do it! Do it!"' said my demons. And I did it. I took the combat stance, just as I had practiced in my hotel room. As he walked past I aimed right at his back and pulled the trigger five times. I remember him sprinting up the stairs, his body turning slowly, jerking forward. The doorman, Jose, I remember him shaking the gun out of my hand. He was crying. He was yelling at me: "Look what you've done! Get out of here. Get out of here." And I said: "Where would I go?"' When police arrived they found Chapman sitting on the pavement reading his beloved - and misinterpreted - 'The Catcher in the Rye'.

He will not be eligible for parole until the year 2000. Chapman says he is talking now because he feels remorse. He claims to have suffered nightmares that he is a visitor in Lennon's home. He said: 'I was talking to Yoko and his sons like a friend of the family. We were all very sad but they understood that I was very sorry for the killing. They understood because they knew that I really didn't mean to kill him. John Lennon was a seeker in the spiritual sense. He knew that a perfect world would never be but he said to just think about it. To have the power to imagine it in the first place is the power to bring us closer to it. The idea is not to hurt everything. The idea is to help everything. I regret that I was the author of this kind of hurt. Perhaps now I can be the author of something helpful.

'It is still very, very difficult to know who I am. There are many times when I just feel utter confusion and pain at being Mark David Chapman.'

'AS HE WALLKED PAST I AIMED RIGHT AT HIS BACK AND PULLED THE TRIGGER FIVE TIMES.'

Above: ***John Lennon and Yoko Ono demonstrate their interpretation of love and peace. Their bizarre public appearance in bed was seen by the youth of the Sixties as a radical and significant statement of pacifism. It was this generation that mourned John's death most strongly.***

Left: ***Police guard the floral tributes left by fans outside the Dakota building where John and Yoko lived.***

RALPH NAU

Love Among the Stars

After Lennon's death, stars began to pay thousands of dollars to protect themselves from 'celebrity stalkers'. Some fans may want only an autograph but madmen like Ralph Nau have robbed the stars of a most precious asset – peace of mind.

America's most deranged celebrity stalker will make his next bid for freedom soon – the same bid he has made every two months since 1989 – but it is a move that sends shivers through Hollywood. Some of America's biggest names fear Ralph Nau, a chilling, deranged killer who has made his life's work an obsessive quest for love among the stars.

He is one of a new brand of fiend bred by America in the latter half of the twentieth century: the tribe of loners and losers who fixate on rich and famous strangers... often loving their heroes to death.

Nau would have stayed a nameless face within America's penal and mental institutions if he had not chosen to prey on famous film stars. He leapt to notoriety in December 1989, when a bevy of celebrities – including Cher and Farrah Fawcett, both of whom had been his victims – blocked his release from a mental institution by revealing that he had bombarded them with letters from behind bars while making bizarre claims that singer Sheena Easton had bought his family farm, that Olivia Newton-John is a murderer, that Madonna is waiting to marry him.

The killing of starlet Rebecca Schaeffer in Hollywood occurred the same year that Cher and Farrah Fawcett stepped forward to complain about Nau and her murder proved their fears regarding Nau's potential release were not unfounded. Schaeffer, just twenty, was a bright, vivacious young girl who had become the obsession of warped loner Robert Bardo, a predator who wasted his life watching daytime soap operas and worthless late-night melodramas . He would later say 'She became my goddess... I worshipped her.' Bardo is serving a life sentence for her murder.

THE BEGINNINGS OF OBSESSION

Ralf Nau is another one of those lonely, lonely people – a man, a psychiatrist once said, who 'wants to assassinate the world'.

At school he was a loner, never able to find a girl to date, or to strike up close friendships with boys his own age. After he left at the age of sixteen, his brother Kerry claimed Ralph joined a club which advertised its services as 'a club to help mature single men find happiness with women.' 'Actually it was a club where one paid a subscription and, in return, received dirty letters through the post.

Ralph paid his money and got letters from 'Candy' that he treasured. He showed these to several people in his hometown of Antioch in Illinois. He was laying the groundwork for his obsession... that it was perfectly possible for people, who had never met, to love each other.

He started writing letters to showbiz stars when he moved to Hollywood in 1980. He began with Cher because he had had a schoolboy crush on her and to another woman named Maria. Ralph said that Maria was 'a sorceress – the magic lady who led me to things with Olivia Newton-John.' It was then that he knew he had to live in California.

OBSESSIVE LOVE, WEAPONS, DEATH, SUICIDE, RELIGION

He signed the first missives to Cher as 'Shawn Newson-John' and put the return address on the back as Xanadu. Initially, the letters were outpourings of love, but then veiled threats began to appear, hinting at what violence he would commit if his love was unrequited.

At home, in his solitary room, he penned more of the sick love letters, adding Sheena Easton, Farrah Fawcett and Madonna to his list. He turned his room into a shrine to Olivia Newton-John and named a dog Sam, after the love song of the same name that was one of her hits.

THESE POOR WRETCHES, BRANDED 'STALKERS' BY THE LEGAL AND MEDICAL WORLD, CAN FORM NO REAL OR WORTHWHILE RELATIONSHIPS.

IT WAS A CLUB WHERE ONE PAID A SUBSCRIPTION AND, IN RETURN, RECEIVED DIRTY LETTERS THROUGH THE POST.

HE WAS A MODEL EMPLOYEE. BUT AT NIGHT, AT HOME, HE CHANGED. IN HIS SOLITARY ROOM, HE PENNED MORE OF THE SICK LOVE LETTERS.

Opposite: ***Ralph Nau revealed his incipient insanity in letters to celebrity women but proved his madness in the murder of his little step-brother.***

But then he had to kill the dog with an overdose of sleeping tablets because, in Ralph's twisted mind, Sam was keeping Olivia away from him.

Diana Ross became a victim. So did Connie Chung, one of America's top newscasters. But Olivia was the main target and he began signing his letters with his real name. Olivia hired a top security firm in Hollywood run by Gavin DeBecker, who though he followed Nau, did not report to the police. DeBecker said 'The criminal justice system is looking for something very clear to commit a man to prison or hospital, like the fact that he struck his mother or bought a gun and pointed it at someone. But here was a guy who went to work every day, who was doing no harm. A court would have laughed us out of the room. Hell, they'd say, who cares if he has a few obsessions about Olivia Newton-John? Who doesn't?'

For the next three years, at Olivia's request, DeBecker and his men monitored virtually every move that Ralph Nau made.

Nau saved his money up to see Sheena Easton and Olivia at concerts in Los Angeles. He travelled to the set of 'Mask' to catch a glimpse of Cher making the movie. And all around him were DeBecker's men, who were now on a twenty-four-hour-surveillance of their most dangerous suspect.

At one Newton-John concert Nau scrambled on to the stage but was hauled off by DeBecker's toughs. 'I knew the concert stopped after I ran away,' he wrote to her later, 'because I know you were only playing for me.' He hung around Cher's movie studio. He stalked Sheena Easton and Farrah Fawcett to their homes. He travelled across America in pursuit of the women who, he was convinced, loved him.

In 1983 the vet's business where he worked was sold and Nau, who neither smoked, drank nor dated, used his savingto fly to Australia to track down Olivia.

He spent a week sleeping in a hired car as he tried to get close to her ranch. Police believe that while he was there, he may have murdered a vagrant, although it was never proved and he was never charged.

Nau returned, dejected to America, and used the last of his savings on a jaunt to Scotland to see Sheena Easton who, he had read somewhere, had returned to her homeland. He was turned back by customs officers who had been informed by DeBecker of the real reason for his visit.

Above: ***Cher was Ralph's 'first love'. He never met her yet was convinced that he enjoyed a relationship with the beautiful and famous stranger.***

HE HAD TO KILL THE DOG WITH AN OVERDOSE OF SLEEPING TABLETS BECAUSE SAM WAS KEEPING OLIVIA AWAY FROM HIM.

Ralph Nau returned home to his father's farm where his family noted, with rising alarm, his ever-more crazy behaviour. He began taking three-hour-long showers with the family dog.

DeBecker rang Ralph's father, and warned him of his son's obsession with celebrities, for Ralph's letters were still pouring in. Delmar Nau contacted a lawyer who said there was little that could be done until Ralph actually harmed someone.

In January, 1984, he sold his beat-up car and with the last of his savings made a second pilgrimage to Australia, in a bid to 'reconcile once and for all' with Olivia. This time DeBecker knew Nau's plans and arranged for the superstar to be away from her ranch. His security people followed Nau every inch of the journey. Ralph wandered around the outback for a week on his own. He never saw Olivia.

Within months he was sitting in a jail on a murder charge. He had axed to death eight-year-old Denis Gerken, his mentally retarded stepbrother. Denis could neither read nor write, could not talk or even dress himself. He was a totally vulnerable child.

When Nau returned from Australia, his parent's marriage was over and his mother, Shirley, had married egg farmer Ken Gerken. Ralph was given a job on Ken's farm and, on a steamy August night, his madness finally overwhelmed him.

When he was being interrogated for the murder, Ralph Nau told the police: 'Olivia sends me messages all the time. She tells me how much she loves me and how much she wants me to be with her. She paid my way back to the United States.

'I think you might find Denny with a dog I buried. Yes, you might find him there...' Police found the little boy's body in a cornfield. There was no dog's corpse.

Psychiatrists at his trial said the boy was killed because he tried to change channels on the TV set as Ralph was watching one of his heroines, Nadia Comaneci, performing. At concerts and film sets and airports, burly security men had stopped Ralph getting close to his ladies and now, here was Denis, stopping him in his own home. The boy had to pay for it with his life.

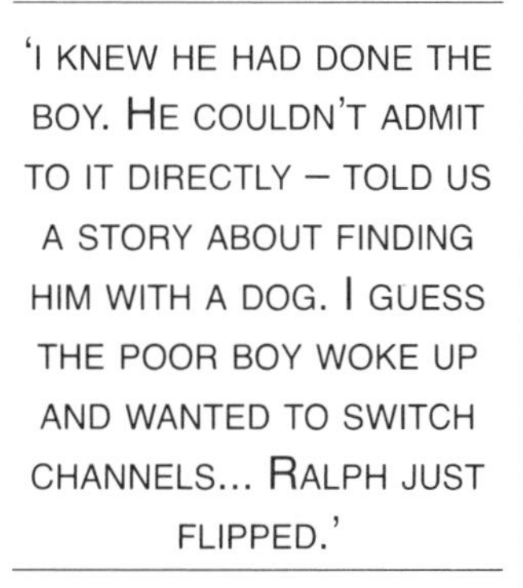
'I KNEW HE HAD DONE THE BOY. HE COULDN'T ADMIT TO IT DIRECTLY – TOLD US A STORY ABOUT FINDING HIM WITH A DOG. I GUESS THE POOR BOY WOKE UP AND WANTED TO SWITCH CHANNELS... RALPH JUST FLIPPED.'

Police said that on the night of 8 August, 1984, Ralph's mother put Denis to bed. She and her husband were watching TV in a family room at one end of the house while Denis was asleep in his room. Ralph was watching TV in the living room. Nadia Comaneci was on and he was spellbound.

THE STARING EYES OF A MADMAN

Around 10pm Ralph told the family that he had heard Denis crying, went to check on him, but then found that he was not there. While the family searched the house and nearby land Ralph hurriedly washed his clothes and cleaned his boots. Sherrifs arrived half-an-hour later and their only suspect was Ralph. 'He has strange, staring eyes,' said Lt Chester Iwan, of the Lake County Sherrif's Department. 'I had to interrogate him. I knew he had done the boy. He couldn't admit to it directly – told us a story about finding him with a dog. I guess the poor boy woke up and wanted to switch channels. Ralph's 'beloved' was on and he just flipped.'

At the Chester Mental Health Facility where he was sent initially, psychiatrists began to realize that Ralph Nau was seriously disturbed. He was confined for just six months before a court ruled that his confession was inadmissible, because he could not be regarded as sane or responsible for his actions. There followed five years of legal wrangling until he was confined, in 1989, to the Elgin Mental Health Centre in Illinois. But the legal system in the United States allows a mental patient the right to apply every sixty days for release from an institution. At every opportunity Ralph Nau applies for his freedom, but his requests are counteracted by the star victims of his letters.

'However, he will be out one day and there are people who may not have the money it takes to hire a DeBecker,' said one disillusioned lawman, who fought to get Ralph Nau sentenced to life imprisonment for the murder of the little boy.

Below: ***Olivia Newton-John, the Australian singer whose life was made a misery by the unwanted attentions of Ralph Nau, a man she had never met. She hired a major security firm to protect herself from the man.***

JOE DOHERTY
IRA Hitman

He grew up in bitterness and with a strong sense that he was a victim. Joe Doherty took his revenge with evil acts of killing and maiming the innocent – all in the name of patriotism.

The murder of a Special Air Services officer in a grubby Belfast street in 1980 would, on the surface, have little connection with the 1986 bombing of Libya's deranged dictator Colonel Gaddafi in Tripoli. One was carried out by a psychopathic Irish Republican Army terrorist called Joe Doherty who dressed up his murderous outrage in the guise of freedom fighter. The other was carried out by trained pilots on the orders of Ronald Reagan, US president, as a warning to Ghaddafi to desist from his global sponsorship of terrorist causes.

Not until 1992, when the fugitive gunman Doherty was finally brought back in chains from America to serve a life sentence for his killing of Captain Herbert Richard Westmacott did the correlation between his murder and the Tripoli bombing raid become clear. For it was Mrs Thatcher, as much as any police officer, intelligence operative and FBI agent whose long arm stretched across the Atlantic to bring Doherty home from America – where he sought political sanctuary – to face justice. Doherty was 'payback' for Tripoli because Mrs Thatcher had allowed US warplanes to take off from British bases on their mission. She weathered a great deal of criticism at the time over the decision and made it plain to her American opposite numbers that, one day, a favour might have to be returned. That favour came in the form of thirty-seven-year-old Joseph Patrick Doherty, the killer that Mrs Thatcher would not let get away.

The story of Joseph Doherty – street-thug, rioter, ambusher, political assassin and propaganda pawn – is an odyssey from the breeding ground of hatred through to the highest levels of international intrigue and diplomacy. If he had chosen another path as a youngster, one away from the gun and the hard men who rule his ghetto area of West Belfast, he might now be a father with a secure job and a bright future. Instead, he will be almost a pensioner when he is finally released. The only value he has to the IRA now is to embellish the memories of 'the cause' when the stories are told around pub fires and in meeting halls where the Republican ethos is worshipped like a religion.

Below: ***A priest kneels by the body of David Howe, killed when he inadvertently blundered into an IRA funeral procession.***

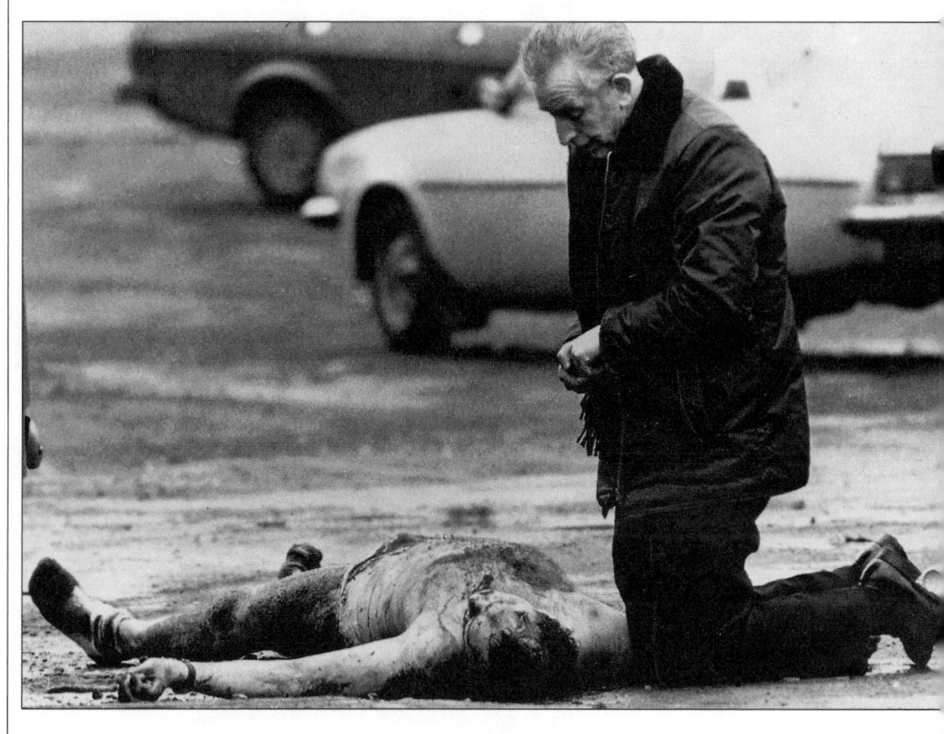

Before he became infamous, Joe Doherty was born into a system that preached and practised unfairness towards the Catholic minority in Northern Ireland. Artificial electoral boundaries, discrimination towards Catholics in schools, housing, jobs and civil rights and terror in the form of the police 'B Specials' combined to fuel the resurgence of the Republican movement that was dormant, if not dying, by the time Doherty was born in 1955, to a family that celebrated Irish rebel heroes in the uprising with Britain in the early part of the century that won the south its independence. Doherty says when he was five he felt the first stirrings of a grave injustice being committed in his country. He said: 'I remember going to school and being taught English instead of our national language. You take the history classes we went to. It

Opposite: ***Joe Doherty, the IRA man who murdered in cold blood, then sought sanctuary in the United States by claiming he was a political refugee.***

Above: ***On the right, the then-Mayor of New York, David Dinkins, his political antennae keenly aware of the massive Irish-American vote in his city, woos the Irish murderer, Joe Doherty. Dinkins was not heard to give sympathy to Irish – or other – victims of Doherty's killing habits.***

Right: ***The reality of the IRA's actions was seen yet again in London when nine soldiers and seven cavalry horses were blown apart by terrorist bombs in Hyde Park in 1982.***

THE GLAMOUR OF THE GUN SOON LURED DOHERTY INTO THE CLUTCHES OF THE IRA.

was mostly on the Tudors and royal heads, kings and queens of England. We were told nothing about our own country. When we took geography we were given the map of England, Scotland and Wales, Europe, the United States, but we were never given a map of our own country. So it was resented by a young person at my age that I couldn't learn where the hell I am living. I knew more about Birmingham and Manchester than I knew about my own city and the beautiful countryside that was around it.' Bitter words from one of the oppressed.

The glamour of the gun soon lured Doherty into the clutches of the IRA, the illegal but best guerilla operation in the world. Involved with petty crime from the age of fourteen – offences like housebreaking and thieving – he joined the organization Na Fianna Eireann, the junior wing of the Provisional IRA. In these early days, with the burning resentment against British troops in his land growing inside him, he was a willing recruit. In the far-flung, remote regions of County Donegal and on the west coast of Ireland, he attended the indoctrination and training sessions that would give him both the spirit and the practical tools to become an effective IRA operative. In this role he became an intelligence scout for the IRA killers on the streets of Belfast; warning of the approach of a police or army patrol, luring soldiers into ambushes and assisting in diversions when terrorists or arms had to be removed from an area rapidly.

He also became a member of the notorious knee-capping squads. These vigilantes were an important factor in IRA rule in the early days of the troubles – patrolling dances and drinking halls, dispensing rough and ready justice to those who they deemed were either drunkards, drug pushers or potential enemies of the IRA. Doherty would later claim that he was little more than a concerned citizen when he carried out these vigilante duties – but he had shown himself, to his IRA superiors, ruthless and efficient – two qualities which they prized very highly indeed.

PRISON LESSONS IN TERRORISM

Doherty's pathological loathing of the British continued to rise as army attempts to root out and contain terrorism spilled over into his own neighbourhood. He witnessed his family being pulled from their beds at midnight by soldiers and was continually quizzed by intelligence officers about his membership of the junior IRA. On 22 January 1972, a day after his seventeenth birthday, he found himself interned without trial at one of the several British camps. He claimed he was tortured in Girdwood camp. While human rights investigators have determined that some terrorists were subjected to cruel and inhuman treatement while in internment camps, not a shred of evidence exists to say that Doherty was mistreated, and certainly he never suffered the use of electric shock apparatus which he claimed was in common use in the camp.

Later he was interned on the prison ship Maidstone and in Long Kesh where IRA cell leaders marked him down as a zealot who would soon be ready for active service in the field – namely, killing people. Inside the camps was a well-organized IRA network that kept prisoners indoctrinated with the lectures on the Republican movement and weapons they would be using on their release. Doherty joined the adult arm of the IRA upon his release, swearing his allegiance to the terrorists in the traditional way; placing his hand upon a Bible, a .45 revolver and the Irish tricolour, he thus became a volunteer in C Company, 3rd Battalion of the Irish Republican Army. During the early Seventies, outfits like Doherty's caused tremendous civilian loss of life with indiscriminate bombings, sectarian murders and numerous shootings of security and police personnel, but he was never charged with any specific murders, although security personnel had plenty of suspicion. The only charge they nailed him on came in 1973 when he served three months for being caught in possession of a starting pistol; a tool he used to intimidate neighbourhood youths.

NOT A SHRED OF EVIDENCE EXISTS TO SAY THAT DOHERTY WAS MISTREATED, AND CERTAINLY NEVER SUFFERED THE USE OF ELECTRIC SHOCK APPARATUS.

Below: ***Another view of the bombing in Hyde Park, where men died like animals and animals died like men.***

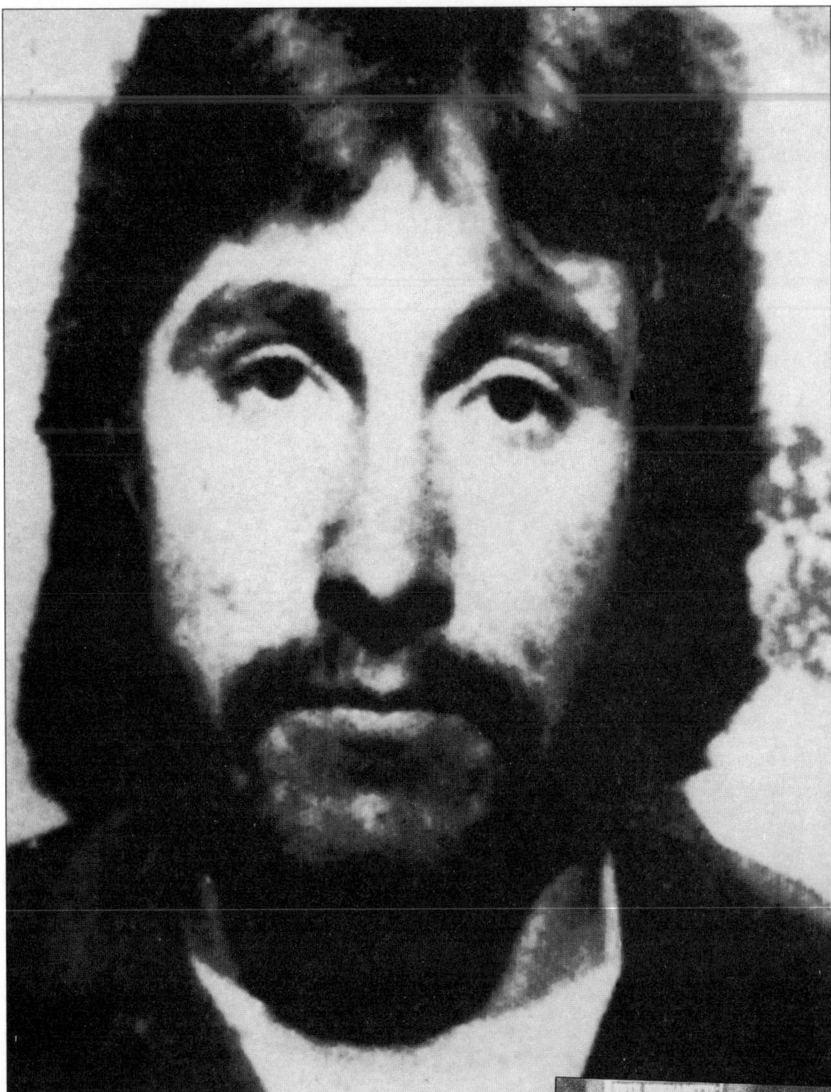

He was released shortly before Christmas 1979 – the last Christmas he would know as a free man. When he was neither a fugative on the run, or a man held behind bars.

MASTERING A LETHAL WEAPON

After he walked free again Joe Doherty was singled out for special training with the M60 heavy machine gun, a fearsome weapon capable of cutting a man in two with a split-second burst. He later denied ever being trained in the handling of these, but an IRA informer told his Special Branch handlers in Ulster that Doherty was so familiar with every nut and rivet of the weapon, that he could break it down and then re-assemble it wearing a blindfold. This gun, one of a batch stolen from an armoury in America, was to play a major part in his designated IRA 'mission' the following year.

His unit was assigned to kill policemen and soldiers by using the high-powered weaponry acquired from America. Again, Doherty and his cohorts were not charged in this period with any offences and, naturally, he has been at pains to play down any of his activities. The incident which would land him with a life sentence for

Upon his release, shortly before Christmas of that year, he was told to report for active duty to the 3rd Battalion. He was ordered to stay 'on the run', avoiding the homes of friends and family in favour of unknown IRA sympathisers, because the IRA had plans for him. In February 1974 he removed eighty pounds of gelignite from one of the organization's dumps and moved it by car to another unit across town. Unfortunately for him an army spot check found him and his portable, unprimed bomb and both were taken into custody. He was given a three-year sentence, compounded shortly afterwards with another eighteen months after a futile prison escape attempt ended in abject failure. In jail he rose in the IRA ranks and was an officer in charge of other men. His masters on the other side of the wire bided their time for Joe Doherty, because they were nurturing big plans.

murder came towards the middle of 1980. His IRA masters chose to mount an attack on a British army patrol – any patrol, it did not matter which – that passed by a house that his unit would take over on the Antrim Road .Doherty knew that military vehicles from the Girdwood base passed by all the time; there was bound to be a rich target. Almost certainly 'blooded' in IRA actions by this time, Doherty and his gang were chosen for the operation on the direct instructions of the leader of the Belfast Brigade of the terror organisation.

Doherty personally planned the operation, ordering that the M60 heavy machine gun was to be fired from one window while the rifles and revolvers used by the gang were positioned at another. He ordered his gang to hijack a vehicle the evening before the ambush in order to transport themselves and their weapons to the scene. He gave orders for the family in a house overlooking the spot where they intended to spring the trap to be held hostage. Both were standard IRA procedures for this kind of assassination. But unknown to Doherty and his allies the eyes of army intelligence were already upon them. Members of the 14th Intelligence Company had, through an IRA informer, learned of the operation planned for 2 May, 1980. A unit of the Special Air Services was given careful instruction to tackle them on the day.

Above, right: ***Police check vehicles for IRA car bombs after the terrorist attack on military bandsmen in Deal in Kent, 1989.***

Above, left: ***The army on full alert during an IRA funeral in Belfast.***

Opposite, above: ***Joe Doherty hid behind a beard and long hair when he fled to the USA.***

Opposite, below: ***Hooded IRA men patrol in Belfast.***

The night before the ambush, a blue Ford Transit van was hi-jacked by volunteers and handed over to Doherty's team and driven to the rear of house number 371 in the Antrim Road – designated for the take-over the next day and the base for the ambush. The following morning nineteen-year-old Rosemary Comerford and her two-year-old son Gerard were alone in the house.

She recalled: 'At 10.30am a knock came on the door and I opened it. Two men were standing there and one of them said they were Irish Republican Army. The man who spoke had a handgun pointing at me. This man said they were going to take over the house and they were going to hold me and my son as hostages. He then took us into the bedroom at the rear of the house. The other man who did not speak remained in the bedroom with us. I could hear the other man moving about. I think the man who stayed in the bedroom with us brought the handgun with him. At about 12.30pm my sister Theresa called and the man who was in the bedroom with me told me to go and see who it was. He told me to let her in and said she'd have to stay in the bedroom with us. My husband Gerard came home and the same thing happened.'

At 2pm that day, as Doherty and his 'freedom fighters' took up positions in the occupied house that gave them the best view on to the anticipated killing zone, Captain Herbert Westmacott, thirty-four, and his men were on their way to the scene. The SAS career veteran and his men were trained precisely for this kind of urban assault. SAS headquarters in England were equipped with houses such as these which Westmacott and his men had neutralized time and time again in their training missions. But a terrible blunder in trying to determine what was the exact entrance to the house gave the gunmen inside vital seconds. The entrance to the house was actually through 369 and not through the door marked 371. Captain Westmacott fell in a pool of blood outside the entrance to 371 after the hitmen inside opened up first. The British government would later charge Doherty, who as he was led away from the scene of the murder said of the M60 that killed Captain Westmacott said: 'that's my baby', with being the triggerman.

Trapped inside like rats Doherty and his men believed they would endure first smoke, then stun grenades before the SAS mounted a charge on their positions that would leave no prisoners. But, as if to disappoint the IRA propaganda machine about such atrocities, they gave the killers inside the kind of chance never afforded to Captain Westmacott. A priest was brought in at Doherty's request to oversee their surrender after the SAS had surrounded them for several hours. Forensic tests taken later on his clothing showed that, of the four-man gang, he had the most ballistic residue on him, indicating that it was probably him who fired the M60 which killed Captain Westmacott.

British interrogators were intent on breaking down Doherty when he was in custody; they knew he was a valued IRA operative who had probably killed before. But he was well versed in the cat-and-mouse games that his handlers had taught him. Every question that was not answered with a refusal was answered with a

CAPTAIN WESTMACOTT FELL IN A POOL OF BLOOD OUTSIDE THE ENTRANCE TO 371 AFTER THE HITMEN IINSIDE OPENED UP FIRST.

Right: ***Airey Neave, on the left, survived the Nazi prisoner-of-war camp at Colditz Castle, only to die in a cowardly IRA killing. They planted a bomb in his car on 30 March, 1979 that killed him the instant he started the vehicle.***

FORENSIC TESTS TAKEN LATER ON HIS CLOTHING SHOWED THAT, OF THE FOUR-MAN GANG, DOHERTY HAD THE MOST BALLISTIC RESIDUE ON HIM.

question. Doherty was a misty-eyed Republican who fondly remembered his grandfather's medals from his time spent fighting the British earlier in the century. He wavered between bravado and mute silence to arrogance and foul language during his interrogation sessions, but he finally cracked when his mother's name was mentioned. He admitted he had tried to get out of the movement but had failed and only wanted a better Ireland to live in. He did not admit to killing Westmacott specifically, only that he had fired a gun.

Above: ***In 1988, a girl walked into an army disco in Mill Hill, North London and laid an IRA bomb. A young man lost his life in the blast.***

Below: ***British soldiers returning to their barracks after home leave in 1988 were blown apart by the IRA. Eight men lost their lives as the bus in which they travelled exploded.***

BACK IN THE BOSOM OF THE IRA

Doherty soon found himself back in the cold familiarity of the Crumlin Road jail after his inquisitors had finished with him. Here he was among familiar faces and old IRA comrades and the bravado that led him to kill easily returned. He was back under the discipline of the IRA where top-level decisions were taken by his masters to turn him into a cross between a martyr and Robin Hood. At the time of the beginning of his trial in April 1987 things were going badly for the IRA leadership; the hunger strike at the Maze prison was claiming lives with five volunteers dead and no sign of the Thatcher government backing down. The leadership of the terror gang badly needed a propaganda break and they saw their opportunity in gaining it with Doherty. He had already refused to recognize the court sitting in justice on him and the fact that he had killed a member of Her Majesty's most elite force ensured that his name was already high up in the newspapers. His leaders instructed him to work on escape plans for him and seven of his fellow inmates.

Doherty handed his commanders their much-needed propaganda victory on 10 June, 1981, when he and seven others made a successful break out from the jail. Using guns smuggled in by IRA sympathisers they overpowered guards – clubbing one brutally – and dressed in prison uniforms to pass a series of checkpoints leading to the staff entrance to the jail. Finally out in the street, a gun battle ensued in a car park between the security forces and the IRA units sent to pick up the escapers. Doherty fled through the warren of streets in the Shankhill area of town – a fiercely loyalist enclave, but nothing happened to him and he was able to reach his own turf unscathed. Once there he was kept away from his family and friends – the first target of searches by the army – and sheltered at the homes of sympathisers who had no record of IRA membership or of terrorist offences. Within days he was moved south of the border into the Irish Republic where he was hidden in an even more remote region. As he bided his time for several months he heard the news from Belfast that Lord Justice Hutton had found him Guilty of murder *in absentia*, sentenc-

ing him to life imprisonment with a recommendation to the Home Secretary that he should serve a minimum of thirty years inside. It did much to take the edge from his fame as 'The Great Escaper' as he was now known among Republican sympathisers. His masters in Belfast knew that his pursuers would leave no stone unturned in their hunt for him and so took the decision to give him a new identity and send him off to America where a massive Irish community – which gave literally millions of dollars each year to the war chests of their fighting units – would ensure his safety as a fugitive. He left Ireland under the name of Henry J. O'Reilly in February 1982... ready to bury himself in anonymity until his overlords called him to service once again when the heat was off.

Margaret Thatcher was not prepared to let the killer of a British officer escape so easily. In his authoritative book on Doherty entitled 'Killer in Clowntown' author Martin Dillon wrote: 'Doherty was a prestige target and, little did he know then, to the British prime minister at the time, Margaret Thatcher. The killing of Westmacott and the escape of his killers angered her. Doherty was the only one unaccounted for and eventually become so important that she would demand to be personally briefed about him. Thatcher believed that his recapture would enhance relations between Britain and Ireland and repair damage to security in Northern Ireland resulting from the 'Great Escape.' Neither the IRA nor Doherty needed to be convinced of her intentions or her determi-

Above: ***Eighteen soldiers were killed when the IRA ambushed a convoy in Warrenpoint, County Ulster in 1979.***

Right: ***Funerals for IRA men are given the importance and ritual suited to matyrs. These men are bearing the coffin of IRA hitman, Brian Mullin.***

HIS MASTERS IN BELFAST KNEW THAT HIS PURSUERS WOULD LEAVE NO STONE UNTURNED AND DECIDED TO GIVE HIM A NEW IDENTITY AND SEND HIM TO AMERICA.

nation to see them fulfilled. But they were unaware then of her growing personal interest in him.'

DOHERTY'S NEW LIFE IN NEW YORK

In New York, Doherty got a job with a construction company while lodging with a family sympathetic to the Republican cause in Ulster. He also worked as a shoe-shine boy, a bell-hop in a hotel and, with a fake social security number, managed to get a job as a barman at Clancy's Bar in Manhattan. Here he earned upwards of $120 per day with tips and thought the going was good. He had a girlfriend, a comfortable apartment in New Jersey and had adapted to life outside the strict discipline of the IRA with ease. He thought he had it made.

But the heat was on in Ireland to get him back. Thatcher, receiving almost weekly intelligence briefings on his suspected whereabouts, gave her Royal Ulster Constabulary chiefs and army intelligence officers but one brief: find him. The Federal Bureau of Investigation in America was contacted in 1983 and a full file sent over to officers in New York listing every physical trait of the wanted man together with a profile of his habits and psychological breakdown. Soon questions were being asked around town among a network of IRA informers and it came to the notice of FBI agent Frank Schulte that there was a young man working at Clancy's Bar who fitted the bill. On 18 June 1983, he was seized at work. Margaret Thatcher was informed later that same day and she thought that he would be home in a matter of days to begin his thirty-year sentence. But it would be many years of tortured manouvreings and murky intrigue before Doherty heard the slam of a British cell door clang behind him.

Below: ***Joe Doherty, healthy, defiant and fighting against an extradition order requested by the British government. Doherty was detained for eight years in custody in the USA during his determined attempts to appeal against the order. He lost his case and was returned to Britain where he resumed a life sentence for murder.***

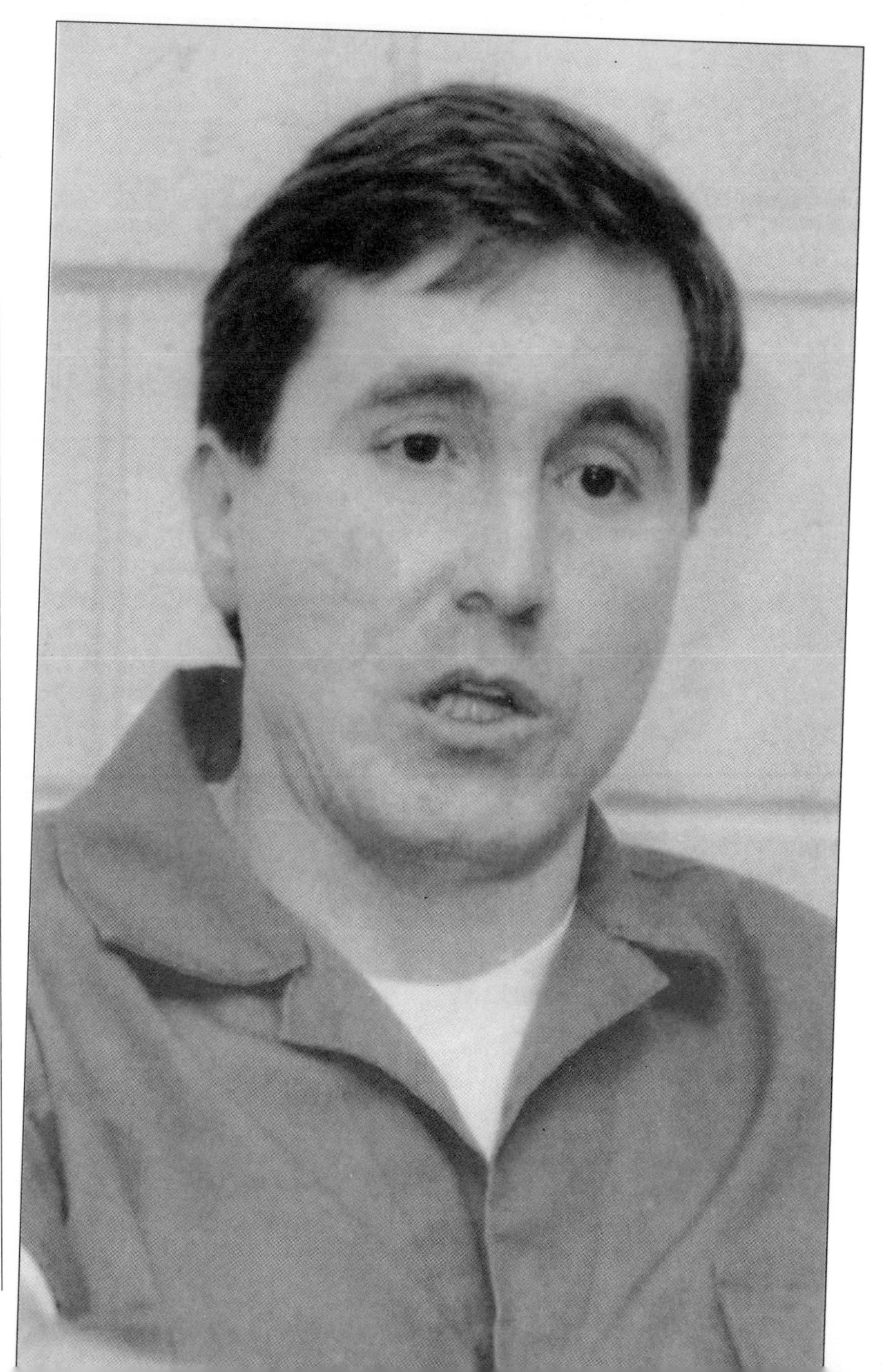

Above: ***The scene of horror at Enniskillen, Northern Ireland, when the IRA slaughtered worshippers at a Remembrance Day service in 1987. Eleven people were killed.***

Joe Doherty found himself in the enviable position of being a hero to a large part of the Irish-American population in New York. To these citizens of the Big Apple he was not the common murderer as depicted by Mrs Thatcher and the British establishment; rather he was a freedom fighter, a hero in the armed struggle to rid Ireland of the English 'oppressor'. He soon found himself with the kind of fame usually reserved for a showbusiness celebrity. Everyone wanted to press Doherty's flesh – the American senator Jesse Jackson was among one hundred politicians who petitioned for him to be granted political asylum in America. Eventually Mayor David Dinkins of New York would come to name the block outside the Manhattan Correctional Centre where he was held 'Joe Doherty Corner.' To Mrs Thatcher and all the victims of IRA terrorism it was the equivalent of re-naming a London street after the Boston strangler for Doherty is also a crude killer.

JOE DOHERTY FOUND HIMSELF IN THE ENVIABLE POSITION OF BEING A HERO TO A LARGE PART OF THE IRISH-AMERICAN POPULATION IN NEW YORK.

Initially Doherty was charged with illegal entry into the USA – he had, after all, committed no crimes in America. Time after time after time courts ordered his release on bail and a full immigration hearing, only to have the legal process blocked from on high. Clearly, the hand of something or someone much bigger than the usual legal process was being brought into play repeatedly. Ronald Reagan, who enjoyed an unusually cozy relationship with Mrs Thatcher, was, like her, a man dedicated to the opposition of terrorism. She expected him to deliver Doherty up to her, but he was thwarted at every turn by the procedures of the US judicial system. In 1986 came the Libyan bombing when Reagan took his own stand against world terrorism by attempting to kill Colonel Gaddafi. Mrs Thatcher stood alone among western leaders by allowing the American warplanes to take off from British bases on their mission. When Britain continued to be frustrated by the American courts Mrs

Thatcher's emissaires diplomatically reminded America that they 'owed' Britain a favour. The favour was Doherty for Tripoli and it was said so by Sherard Cowper Coles, a senior British diplomat, to Otto Obermaier, US attorney assigned to prosecuting him. He told Obermaier: 'The prime minister believes you owe us this one. She allowed your government to use our territory for your F1-11s when they were on their way to bomb Tripoli.'

But the legal process ground on and on in Doherty's favour. The American court system, examining the statues of the constitution of the United States and every similar case that had gone before, could not find sufficient arguments to warrant the deportation of Doherty. At one bail hearing in September 1990, after he had won over a dozen court cases that kept being referred to higher and higher authorities, Doherty gave a classic terrorist's 'doublespeak' account for his killing of Westmacott. He said: 'It was to bring pressure on the British government, to force them to negotiations. That was the reason I was involved in the operation, to bring to the British government that their presence in the North of Ireland is unworkable, politically and militarily, and that they cannot suppress the IRA, that the IRA can survive and strike back.' This from a man who lied to the American courts that he had left the organization in 1982.

TIME AFTER TIME AFTER TIME COURTS ORDERED HIS RELEASE ON BAIL AND A FULL IMMIGRATION HEARING, ONLY TO HAVE THE LEGAL PROCESS BLOCKED FROM ON HIGH.

THE SUPREME COURT REJECTED ANY FURTHER HEARINGS

By 1992 he was the longest held political prisoner, held without a charge other than that he had come into the country illegally, in America. There was still intense pressure on the White House – now under the occupancy of the Bush administration – from No.10 Downing Street, whose keys had passed to John Major. By February 1992 Joe Doherty's case reached the highest court in the land, the Supreme Court. He prayed for an immigration hearing, a separate tribunal that might allow him the political sanctuary he craved. But, almost nine years after he had first been arrested and locked up, it ended for him. The Supreme Court rejected any and all further hearings. On 19 February they came for him – as he rightly predicted they would – to, in his own words, 'complete my sentence in the hell of a British prison.' Doherty was taken from a new lock-up in Kentucky and flown to Northern Ireland where IRA men in Belfast's Crumlin Road jail, scene of his great escape, welcomed him with cake and tea.

The saga of Joe Doherty ended in complete victory for Mrs Thatcher and the opponents of terrorism everywhere. Doherty's supporters, and particularly his lawyer in America, Mary Pike, argued that the American judicial system had been bent, perverted to the cause of Britain and not the interests of the Stars and Stripes.

However, one senior British diplomat, who wishes to remain anonymous, said: 'He was a top operative before he got caught and he tried to con the people of America that he had seen the senselesness of violence, that he had reformed.

'He cannot complain of dirty tricks because he formerly employed every one in the book. Yes, America did owe Britain one for Tripoli – and now the debt has been repaid in full.'

Below: ***Mrs Thatcher was guarded by a young marine as she went to show her respects to the dead bandsmen in Deal, Kent. She called the IRA terrorists 'monsters' and was relentless in her fight against them.***

CARLOS THE JACKAL
The Supreme Terrorist

As a boy he was trained in hatred; as an adult he has terrorised the entire globe with his murderous acts. Yet Carlos the Jackal has never been caught and the whereabouts of one of the world's most wanted men remains a mystery.

He has written his name in blood across the world. A master of disguise, an expert urban guerilla, a killer without compunction or compassion, he moves at ease within the terror networks who support him or hire him, with a slush fund of ready cash and an inexhaustible supply of passports. At various times in various places, he has gone under the names of Carlos Andres Martinez-Torres, Hector Lugo Dupont, Cenon Marie Clarke, Adolf Jose Muller Bernal, Flick Ramirez, Glenn Gebhard and Ahmed Adil Fawaz. His real name is Illyich Ramirez Sanchez. But to police forces all over the globe he is known simply as Carlos the Jackal.

This master of global terrorism is as elusive as he is infamous. Interpol dragnets, complex deals within deals of the diplomatic and espionage worlds, and operations masterminded by the world's leading anti-terrorist units have failed to flush him out and bring him to justice for his crimes – crimes that include the attempted assassination of Joseph Sieff, head of Marks and Spencer; the murder of two French counter-espionage agents; the mass kidnap of OPEC delegates in Vienna; car bombings in France that claimed five people; the machine-gun massacre at Israel's Lod Airport which claimed twenty-five lives; and rocket attacks on aircraft at a Paris airport.

This bloody killer, who mocks the combined efforts of the civilized world to capture him, comes from simple roots. Born in 1949 in Venezuala, he was the son of a left-wing lawyer who admired Stalin. Instead of nursery rhymes and picture books, Carlos grew up on a diet of orthodox Marxist-Leninism. His father believed violent, global revolution was the only lesson worth teaching and by the time he was a teenager, Illyich – named after Vladimir Illyich Ulyanov, Lenin's real name – was a willing disciple of his father's beliefs. Clever, dispassionate, Carlos believed in the overthrow of world capitalism, and he identified with the minorities of the world. The IRA in Ulster, the Palestinians in Israel, the ETA terrorists in the Basque region of Spain – these were the heroes of the young Carlos. When he was seventeen, his father packed him off to a terrorist training camp in Cuba.

THIS BLOODY KILLER, WHO MOCKS THE COMBINED EFFORTS OF THE CIVILIZED WORLD TO CAPTURE HIM, COMES FROM SIMPLE ROOTS.

Above: ***Scene after the 1983 terror bombing of the US Marine base in Beirut which many suspect was master-minded by Carlos.***

Opposite: ***Carlos the Jackal, master of disguise and ruthless terrorist.***

At the camp near Havana, Carlos learned the rudiments of handling explosives, unarmed combat and weaponry. In the latter field he was particularly adept, proving himself a crack shot with any calibre of weapon from a pistol to an automatic rifle. He also developed a thorough disregard for human life which served him well in his chosen profession. One of his instructors gave an interview to a Paris newspaper several years later: 'He was clinically detached from everything he did, mechanical, a superb pupil to train. You could tell from the way he pulled a trigger or pulled down an opponent on the judo mat that there was no emotion attached to anything. It was all just business for him.'

After his initial training in terrorism in Cuba, he was shipped to London where he lived briefly with his mother – estranged from his father – at addresses in Wimpole Street and the King's Road, Chelsea. His brother Lenin – his real name – was with him during this time, around 1968, and the two of them spent endless hours with anarchists in bars where they talked about changing the world through violence. In 1969, Carlos moved on again – this time to the 'finishing school' for terrorists, the Patrice Lumumba Friendship University in Moscow. This seat of learning was in reality the world's top terror academy. Within its walls the Soviets trained some of the most diabolical killers in the world, all of them intent on changing society to fit in with the Marxist-Leninist doctrine.

Opposite, top: ***Carlos pictured at a cocktail party in London in the Seventies. He is with his mother and a girlfriend.***

Opposite, bellow: ***The collection of arms and ammunition that Carlos left behind when he fled a Paris flat.***

2

FILIACION
PERSONAL DESCRIPTION

Cédula de Identidad
Identification Card 6365201

Nacionalidad
Nationality CHILENA

Nacido el
Date of birth 1- JULIO - 1947

Estado civil
Marital status SOLTERO

Profesión
Profession INGENIERO

Domicilio
Address PEDRO TORRES 360

Observaciones
Notes

Nº 035848 1971 3

FILIACION
PERSONAL DESCRIPTION

REGISTRO CIVIL E IDENTIFICACION DE QUILLOTA Dopto. de Quillota CHILE

DIGITO PULGAR
THUMB PRINT

FIRMA DEL TITULAR
SIGNATURE OF BEARER

Above: ***A false passport found in a Paris flat after French law officers had been shot by Carlos.***

Here he learned about the various guerilla groups who needed help and were willing to pay for it. From the Middle East to the killing fields of Asia, from the back alleys of Belfast to the sun drenched plains of Spain's Basque region, there were wars for 'freedom' by minority groups. Also at Patrice Lumumba, he forged contacts that were to be invaluable to him, and he mastered the intricacies of the world banking system. This latter lesson was to serve him well when he began to procure arms and secure payment for his own terrorist operations.

He spent a year here before he was dismissed for 'riotous and dilettante behaviour.' But western intelligence experts regard this cumbersome phrase as a feint dreamed up by the spy lecturers in order to fool the west that Carlos was never going to be part of international terrorism. Equipped with his new, lethal knowledge, he wrote a letter to his father : 'I am ready for what I must do. Thank you for pointing me on the true and correct path.'

Red Army terrorist, Kozo Okamoto, to lead a kamikaze-squad of terrorists in one the most heinous acts of terrorism ever perpetrated against innocent people. Okamoto and two others were flown to Israel on an Air France flight from Rome. In Rome they checked in luggage packed with automatic weapons and grenades – luggage which in those innocent days of air travel was not checked. Upon arrival in Israel, Okamoto and his accomplices, Rakeshi Okudeira and Yoshuyiki Yasuda, opened their luggage and began spraying the crowded terminal with automatic weapons fire, and hurling grenades into the lines of passengers. A defective grenade accounted for one terrorist, a second was shot by a policeman. Okamoto, who had intended to die in the assault, was knocked to the ground by an El Al maintenance worker as he aimed his machine gun at aircraft on the tarmac. On that dark day, 30 May, twenty-four people died, four more died from their wounds in hospital and seventy-six were wounded, many seriously. It was Carlos' grand opening venue on the stage of world terrorism.

He was paid £1 million for organizing the successful killing mission and his name – taken from the title of 'The Day of the Jackal', the Frederick Forsyth novel about

A BLOODTHIRSTY CREW

He spent some time in Paris with a cell of the Popular Front for the Liberation of Palestine, the PFLP, whom he had befriended in Moscow. He would become the leader of this bloodthirsty crew when the Israeli secret service assassinated its head. The first outrage committed by him is believed to be a bomb aboard a Swissair plane bound for Tel Aviv from Zurich on 21 February, 1970. The bomb exploded within minutes of take-off in the baggage hold, causing a massive fire which brought the jetliner down, killing all two hundred people on board. But Carlos revealed his masterly flair for planning when he organized a 'big target' as he referred to the 1972 massacre at Israel's Lod Airport.

Thanks to the contacts he made in Moscow, Carlos employed the Japanese an assassin stalking Charles de Gaulle – was widely broadcast in terrorist circles as a man who gets things done. Next, Carlos turned his sights on a prominent Jewish figure in Britain; Joseph Sieff, boss of the Marks and Spencer stores and a prominent supporter of Israel. But Carlos botched the assassination and, six years later, he discussed it in a newspaper interview given to a French journalist for the Parisian-based Arabic publication Al Watan Al Arabi. The two men met at a secret hideout in the Middle East and Carlos erroneously referred to Mr Sieff as Lord throughout his interview and said he had been chosen to die 'because he was the most important Zionist in Britain.' Carlos elected to carry out the assasination himself because of his expertise with small arms weapons.

THE ATTEMPTED MURDER OF SIEFF WAS THE ONLY MISSION THAT CARLOS IS EVER KNOWN TO HAVE BOTCHED.

His first operation in England started on 30 December, 1973. Here is how Carlos described it: 'I drove to the Lord's home, parked my car, rang the bell and held the butler at gunpoint. It was 6.45 in the evening. I ordered the butler to call out for his master from the bathroom. The butler did so and fainted. When Lord Sieff opened the bathroom door I fired my old Beretta. He was wounded at the upper lip below the nose. I usually fire three times around the nose. It's sure death. But in Lord Sieff's case only one bullet went off, though I fired three times. When Lord Sieff survived I decided to try again. But by the time I managed to get the necessary weapons two weeks later he had gone off to Bermuda.' The attempted murder of Sieff was the one and only mission that Carlos is ever known to have botched.

In 1974, he struck at the Hague in Holland. He again used Japanese Red Army fanatics for this mission. The terrorists seized the French ambassador and his staff and held them hostage, while Carlos demanded the release of another Red Army terrorist held in Paris. To prove he was not bluffing, and to stave off any 'cheating' from the governments he was blackmailing, Carlos bombed the Drugstore Publics in St Germain-des-Pres in the heart of Paris, killing two and injuring thirty. In the same interview with the Arab paper in which he boasted of the attempted killing of Sieff he said: 'The French authorities

Above: ***Captives taken from OPEC's headquarters in Vienna by Carlos' terror gang are forced to board an aircraft to Algeria.***

panicked. A Boeing 707 was sent to Holland along with the freed Red Army terrorist to pick up the embassy assailants in the Hague. The operation succeeded completely.' Carlos was boastful.

ELUSIVE AND EFFICIENT

By now the western intelligence agencies were building up a profile of this master terrorist. They knew he was based in Europe, but he never stayed in one place long. He was as elusive as he was efficient. The French authorities came close to capturing him, when on 27 June, 1975, a Lebanese informer of the PFLP led two agents of the French Direction de la Surveilance du Territoire to Carlos' apartment in the centre of the city. Michel Mourkabel, the informer, had been at one time Carlos' liason man with the PFLP leadership in the Middle East. Carlos described what happened when Mourkabel brought agents Jean Donatini, thirty-four, and Raymond Dous, fifty-five, to his apartment on the third-floor of a block on the Rue Toullier in the Latin quarter of the city. Carlos has always claimed that there were three French agents present, although the authorities have only ever admitted to two agents. Carlos said to the Arabic newspaper journalist: 'It was 8.45 in the evening when they knocked on the door. I was with two Venezualans and a student girlfriend. One of the Venezualans opened the door and shouted "police." '

'We asked the policeman to have a drink with us. They sat for a while and asked for our passports. We produced them and then they started questioning me about Moukarbel. I denied that I had ever met him. But they said he told them that he knew me and that he was waiting outside to identify me. I then challenged them to

Above: ***Israelis celebrate their successful raid on terrorists who held an aeroplane and its passengers hostage at Entebbe, Uganda.***

HE NEVER STAYED IN ONE PLACE LONG. HE WAS AS ELUSIVE AS HE WAS EFFICIENT.

bring him in. They consulted among themselves and then one of them went out. Fifteen minutes later Moukarbel was brought in. When he started to point his finger at me I realised I had to shoot it out. I realised I had to execute the death sentence. I whipped out my Russian-made pistol and fired first at Donatini who was going for his gun. He was reputed to be a fast marksman. But I was faster and slugged a bullet into his left temple. Then I shot Dous between his eyes. Then I put a bullet under the ear of the third Frenchman. Only Michel was left. He moved towards me, covering his face with his hands. He must have realised at that moment that he who cracks in this field of action is bound to be executed. These are the rules of the game. When he was almost at point-blank range I fired between his eyes. He slumped. I fired a second bullet into his left temple and then raced out into the darkness through the neighbouring apartment. The whole operation took six seconds.'

Carlos fled to London where he holed up with beautiful revolutionary, Nydia Tobon,

Below: ***Marines lay a dead comrade on a stretcher after the massive Beirut bombing, probably organised by Carlos, that took two hundred American lives.***

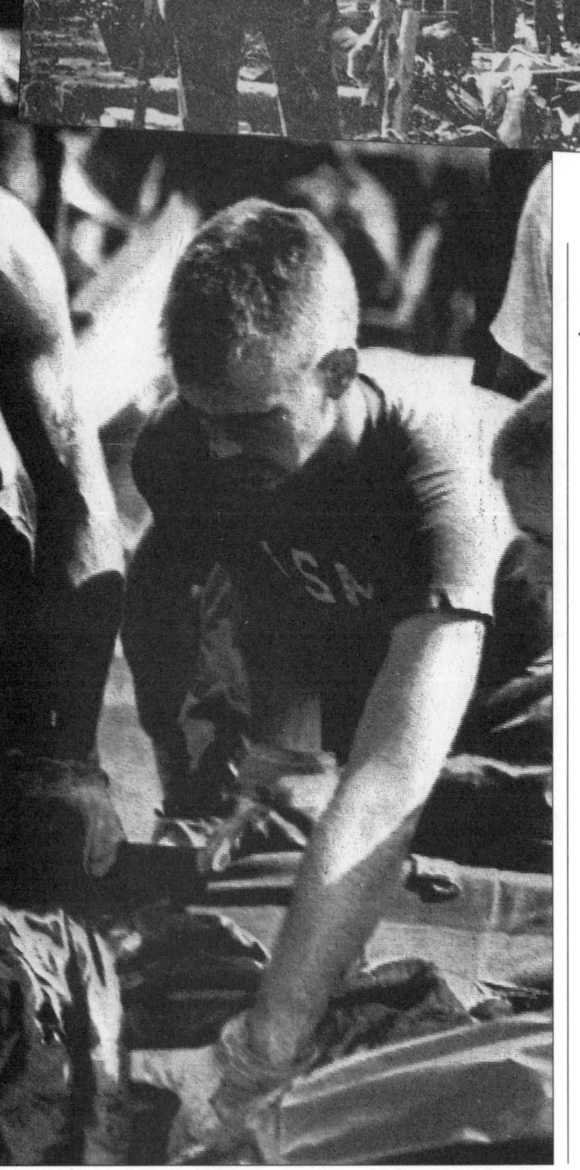

Above: ***Rescuers dig through the rubble, looking for survivors, after the US Marine base was blown up during the troubles in the Lebanon.***

'CARLOS WANTED TO KILLTHE COP. I TOLD HIM TO USE A BIT OF CHARM INSTEAD.'

when police raided the Hereford Road, Bayswater, apartment he had previously shared with twenty-three-year-old Spanish waitress Angela Otaola. They found a cache of arms and in one of the suitcases stashed with weapons, was a shopping list of death. Among the prominent members of British society on the list were Lord and Lady Sainsbury, Sir Keith Joseph, Sir Bernard Delfont and violinist Yehudi Menuhin. Later, Carlos was stopped on the M4 motorway near Reading by Thames Valley police. Tobon, who was expelled from Britain two years after the incident, returned to her native Columbia where she said: 'He had been driving way too fast and we were stopped. The policeman came over and he reached for his pistol. He wanted to kill the cop. I told him to use a bit of charm instead and he let him go with a warning. In the back of the car he had several more weapons and at least eight passports.' Carlos had luck on his side.

In December of the same year Carlos pulled off his most daring exploit.

Working for the PFLP, Carlos masterminded and led a team of daring guerillas in an assault on the OPEC delegates, assembled in Vienna for a conference on world petroleum pricing. Eighty-one delegates of rich Middle Eastern states were present on 21 December when Carlos and his fanatics struck. The PFLP were angry at what they regarded as an Arabic 'sell-out' by states to the 'imperialist' Americans who gave so much support to their arch-enemy Israel. There was an element of that to it, but the main purpose of the mission was to raise funds for future operations – and to line the Swiss bank account of Carlos, Illyich Ramirez Sanchez.

The OPEC meeting was in its second day when Carlos, accompanied by two West German terrorists linked with the Baader-Meinhof gang, two Palestinians and a Lebanese burst into the meeting hall after a shootout with Austrian security guards. They killed three people, including the Libyan delegate to the conference, a bad move, as Libya was one of Carlos' main weapons suppliers, a policeman and an Iraqi employee of that nation's delegation and they wounded seven.

THE MEN WERE RELEASED INTO THE DESERT AFTER AN ESTIMATED 50 MILLION DOLLARS WAS PAID IN RANSOM.

A SAFE PASSAGE OUT OF AUSTRIA

The terrorist gang then seized dozens of hostages, among them Sheik Yamini and Jamshid Amouzegar, Iranian Minister of the Interior. Responsibility for this attack was claimed by the Arm of the Arab Revolution, but it was in reality a PFLP operation. Carlos demanded massive amounts of ransom cash for several of the wealthier delegates and a safe passage for his gang out of Austria. One of the gang members who was wounded by return fire in the initial storming of the conference was treated at a city hospital and returned to Carlos. In return for the freedom of forty-one Austrian hostages the government allowed Carlos to fly out with his hostages from Iraq, Saudi Arabia, Gabon, Ecuador, Venezuala, Nigeria and Indonesia. They flew to Algiers and from there to Libya and the men were eventually released into the desert after an estimated $50 million was paid in ransom by the hostages' nations. It was a stunningly

Below: ***One of Carlos' men was wounded in the OPEC seige in Vienna. He was furious that the authorities removed the man to give him medical care.***

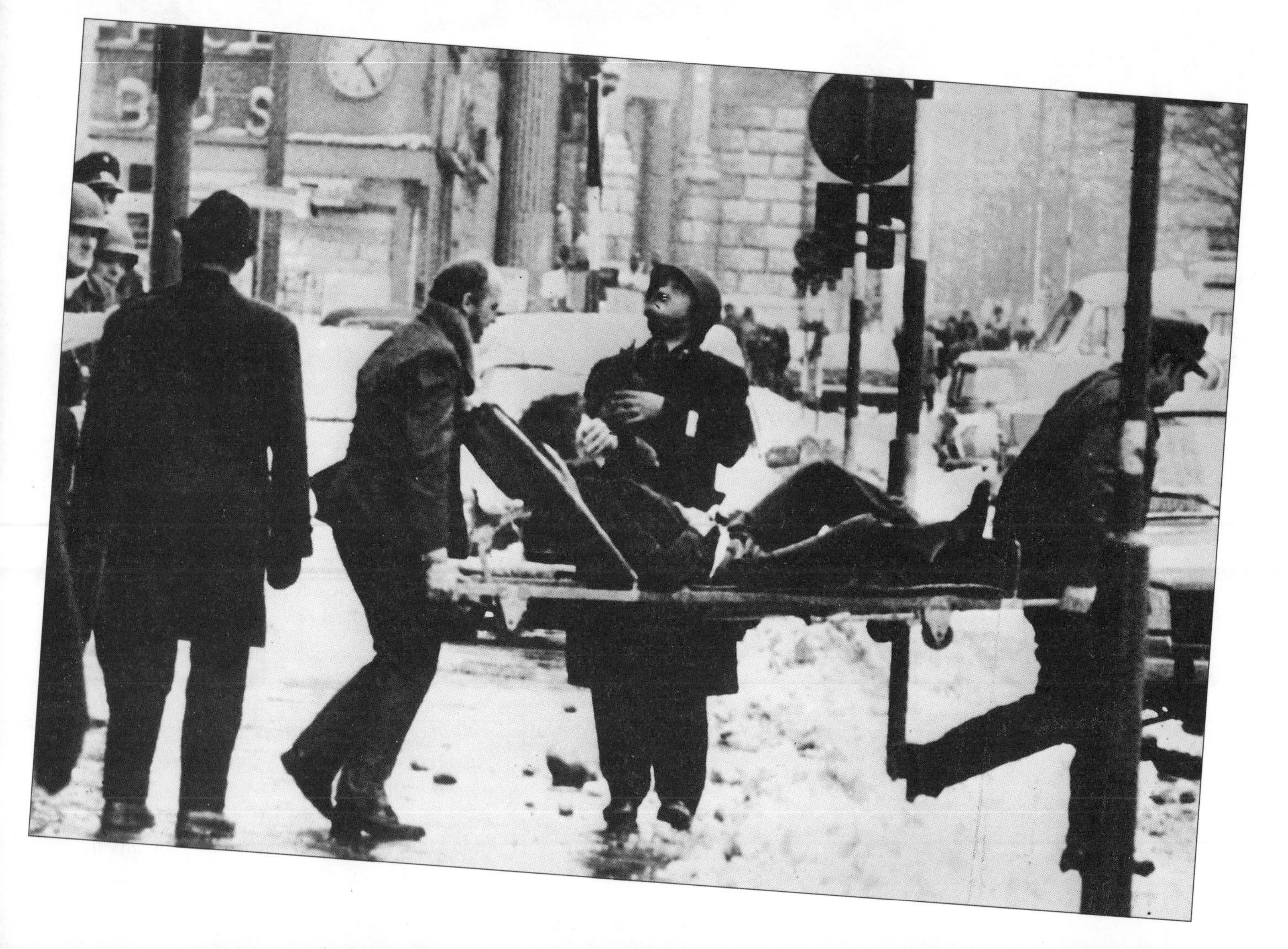

brilliant terrorist operation thanks to the masterful cunning of Carlos.

In the following months he committed a string of assassinations across the world, including the murders of a dissident Syrian exile, a Palestinian rival guerilla leader and several PFLP commanders who needed to be 'purged' from the movement. After resting in a guerilla training camp in Libya, he masterminded, in 1976, the hijacking of an Air France jet en route from Tel Aviv to Paris with two hundred and fifty–eight passengers on board. The plane was diverted and hi-jacked in order to obtain the release of imprisoned terrorists, among them the crazed Okamoto who had caused such carnage at Lod Airport. The hijacked plane landed at Entebbe in Uganda, where Israeli commandos stormed the parked aircraft and released the hostages in a brilliant display of anti-terror tactics. Carlos was said to be angry that the terrorists he sub-contracted for the operation were 'not up to the task'.

After the Entebbe fiasco, Carlos faded into some obscurity. He began training guerillas for Gaddafi in Libya and was said by intelligence agencies to be, at various times, in East Berlin, in Syria, in Czechoslovakia, Iraq, South Yemen and Hungary. He was a man admired for his cool skill but derided by his fellow murderers as a vain, egotistical urban warrior who spent hours on personal grooming. Hans Joachim-Klein, the terrorist badly injured in the OPEC operation, gave an interview to a German newspaper in 1978: 'He was mocked, certainly by his German accomplices, for his vanity. He was always taking showers and powdering himself from head to foot. But no-one could fault him professionally although he did upset

Opposite, left: Carlos as he appeared in a 'wanted' poster after he killed two lawmen in Paris.

Opposite, right: Sheik Yamani, the Saudi Arabian oil minister who was furious that Carlos had sabotaged his meeting in Vienna.

Above: ***Terrorist Hans-Joachim Klein, wanted in connection with the OPEC assault, in a car with the French philosopher, Jean-Paul Sartre (front of car) and left wing lawyer, Klaus Croissant. The urban terrorists attracted some unexpected support.***

HIS MURDERS WERE PLANNED TO COINCIDE WITH THE THIRTIETH ANNIVERSARY OF THE FOUNDING OF THE STATE OF ISRAEL.

several with his constant attempts to take over German revolutionay groups that had nothing to do with him. He was very cool during the whole OPEC operation – he even rode the tram to the hall with all his weapons.' And always well-groomed.

In May 1978 Carlos surfaced in London where he was spotted in Notting Hill by a man working for a foreign embassy in London. Scotland Yard's anti-terrorist branch was put on full alert and the Notting Hill area of the city, where he was seen, was combed, but he was not found. There is speculation that he came to fulfill the contracts on several of the people on the death list drawn up years earlier, and his murders were planned to coincide with the thirtieth anniversary of the founding of the state of Israel.

A WORLDWIDE TERROR CAMPAIGN

When Israel launched the 1982 invasion of Beirut for a full and final reckoning with the Palestine Liberation Organization Carlos hired himself out to Hezbollah fanatics. He is credited with numerous assassinations committed at this time, including the killing of fifty-eight people at the French military headquarters in Beirut.

His last known mission happened just before the outbreak of the Gulf War in 1991. Intelligence sources say Carlos was summoned to Bagdhad by Saddam Hussein and asked to organize a world-wide terror campaign if the West resorted to military action to free Kuwait from the Iraqi invasion. Carlos was alledgedly offered $10 million to organize the terror squads, but pressure was put on him by Syrian and other Arab governments to stay out of this one. Many Arab nations that he had worked for in the past were actually allied with the West against Saddam. Carlos backed out, reputedly with a million-dollar 'consultancy fee' in his back pocket.

Apart from the crimes he is known to have masterminded and committed, he is wanted for questioning on many, many more. His bloody handprints are seen in the murder of Swedish premier Olaf Palme and in the murder of more than two hundred US Marines in Beirut. But with the ruthlessness and cunning he displays, and the number of nations in the world willing to give terrorists refuge, it is highly unlikely that Carlos the Jackal will ever be brought to justice.

His nest is nicely feathered with booty from his bloody games and he may find retirement easier to enjoy than the danger of his terrorist existence. He is reported to have travelled in November 1991, on a Yemeni passport, to Yemen after a falling out with Colonel Gaddafi over the political direction of terrorism. It is believed that Carlos is living with Magdalene Kopp, a Baader-Meinhoff terrorist that he somehow found time to marry at some point during his bizarre international odyssey of death and mayhem.

But perhaps there is a kind of justice waiting for Carlos – the same kind of justice that he himself has dispensed without mercy. According to America's CIA, there is a group of wealthy Arab businessmen which has put out a contract on his head. Aware that fanatics like Carlos pose a threat to everyone in any society, these men are said to have pooled millions of dollars that will go as a reward to the person who assassinates Carlos. But international terror expert, David Funnel, said in Washington: 'It will take a killer of very high calibre indeed to catch Carlos. He has been schooled for too long and is too wily to allow himself to become vulnerable. If his antennae sense danger, he will uproot from one spot and move to another. He is that clever and that cunning.'

'IT WILL TAKE A KILLER OF VERY HIGH CALIBRE INDEED TO CATCH CARLOS.'

Below: ***Red Army guerilla, Kozo Okamoto, the killer who opened fire on the crowds at Lod Airport, Israel, in 1980. He was freed for an exchange of Israeli prisoners in a deal between the Palestinians and Israel.***

HAUPTMANN
The Lindbergh Kidnaping

America wept when the darling child of their aviator hero was kidnapped and murdered. The criminal was tracked down and caught by a brilliant piece of detection, yet he denied his horrible guilt right up to the end.

Stormin' Norman Schwarzkopf was the man of the moment with the US people as he led the allied armies on the road to victory in Operation Desert Storm. But over fifty years before this campaign, it was his father in the glare of publicity. Colonel Norman Schwarzkopf was the head of the police force that investigated the snatching of little Charles Augustus Lindbergh, the son of famed Atlantic solo flier Charles Lindbergh. The kidnapping, and subsequent murder of the little boy, arouses passions to this day. From the time the crime was committed until the day that the kidnapper 'fried' in the electric chair, was four years. Even now, the memory of what befell the son of one of America's great heroes, tweaks the conscience of the nation. Crime expert John Rowland wrote: 'In all countries there are a few criminal cases which have stirred the nation. The British case of this kind was probably Jack the Ripper, the French case was probably that of Landru, the German case probably that of Troppmann. If anyone in the USA is asked what case has created the greatest stir it is what the British press called the 'Lindbergh Baby Case'. It is a tragic story.

Charles Lindbergh caught the imagination of the world when he flew solo over the Atlantic for thirty-three hours in 1927 in his little plane 'The Spirit of St. Louis'. He was honoured in fifty countries around the world. At home, he was more celebrated, more revered than the movie stars who were the true demi-gods of society. Lindbergh could not move anywhere in America without being mobbed, and without his private life being discussed. It was because of this that Charles Lindbergh sought seclusion in the New Jersey town of Hopewell. Situated in Hunterdon County, it was near enough to New York to be convenient for travel and business meetings, and secluded enough to keep sightseers and the ravening hounds of the media away.

'IF ANYONE IN THE USA IS ASKED WHAT CRIMINAL CASE CAUSED THE GREATEST PUBLIC STIR, IT IS THE LINDBERGH CASE.'

But its very location made it the perfect place for a crime – the crime of kidnap. On 1 March, 1932, Charles Lindbergh Jnr was taken from the country mansion and never seen again.

Colonel Lindbergh and his wife Anne retained an apartment in Manhattan and always telephoned the baby's nursemaid, Betty Gow, when they intended returning to their country house. On the night of the kidnapping, the Lindberghs and Gow dined

Above: ***Charles Lindbergh, the aviator hero who was the first man to fly across the Atlantic. This picture shows him in front of his plane before he took off.***

Opposite: ***Bruno Hauptmann in his cell hours before his execution.***

together after the twenty-month-old baby was put to bed at 8pm. The Colonel heard what he decsribed as a 'queer, crackling noise' as he sat in the sitting room after dinner, but dismissed it as something Mrs Gow had dropped in the kitchen, where she was speaking with Mr and Mrs Whateley, an English couple who acted as butler and housekeeper to the family.

At 10pm Betty Gow went up to the nursery to look in on the child. He was gone, but the woman was not unduly worried, believing that her mistress had come in and taken the tot into her room as she often did. When she saw Mrs Lindbergh, however, the panic alarms went off. The mother had not been into see her child and had definitely not removed him to her room. As all five people in the mansion now began a frantic search, it was Colonel Lindbergh who found the heartbreaking note – the note that would feature so prominently in the sensational kidnap and murder trial. Pinned to the radiator and contain some gross spelling mistakes, it read: 'Dear Sir!

'Have $50,000 ready, $25,000 in $20 bills 15,000 in $10 bills and 10,000 in $5 bills. After 2-4 days we will inform you were to deliver the Mony. We warn you for making anyding public or for notify the Police the chld is in gute care. Indication for all letters are signature and 3 holds.'

Close to the signature was a combination of perforations, leading police to believe the semi-illiterate fiend meant holes, not holds. Colonel Lindbergh made one more frantic search of the grounds outside, hoping to see some clue as to which direction his son had been taken, then ran back into the house and immediately telephoned the police. Detectives were on the scene within thirty minutes.

Below: ***These photographs show the glamorous good looks of the aviator, Charles Lindbergh. He was, however, a modest man who disliked publicity. His life was cruelly shattered by his fame which attracted not only applause but also tragedy.***

SCANT CLUES INDEED

Initial inspections discovered footprints of yellow clay in the nursery and the indentation of a ladder in the flower bed below the nursery window – obviously the kidnapper's means of entry into the house. A carpenter's chisel was found half-buried in the soft mud – it had rained for days prior to the kidnapping – and there were ladder scuff marks on the whitewashed wall of the house. But these were scant clues indeed. Within forty-eight hours, President Hoover himself had become involved. Because of the fame of Colonel Lindbergh, and the dastardly nature of the crime perpetrated against him, Hoover ordered the FBI to provide limitless assistance to the New Jersey police. The investigation was headed by Colonel Norman Schwarzkopf who cancelled all police leave in a bid to get the case wrapped up quickly. Neither he, nor anyone else, could conceive that it would be four long years before justice was done.

Experts called in to examine the note speculated that the villain was German or Scandinavian – the spelling of 'gute' and 'anyding' pointed in this direction. The ink was analysed, but found to be a commercial brand easily available right across America, as was the paper it was written on. After questioning the servants, delving into their backgrounds and the ethnic make-up of their families, the police investigation did not move forward one inch. There came a tearful plea from Colonel Lindbergh himself. Ignoring the kidnappers' demands not to tell the police, which in turn meant keeping silent to the public, he published an appeal in big city newspapers across the USA, begging that his son be treated well and safely returned. His wife, in turn, managed to get the newspapers, which her husband had once loathed with such venom, to print details of the baby's diet. It was a special diet for the boy, as he had recently been unwell.

Below: The baby Lindbergh, Charles Jnr., on his first birthday. He was adored by his parents and his father described him as 'the perfect son.'

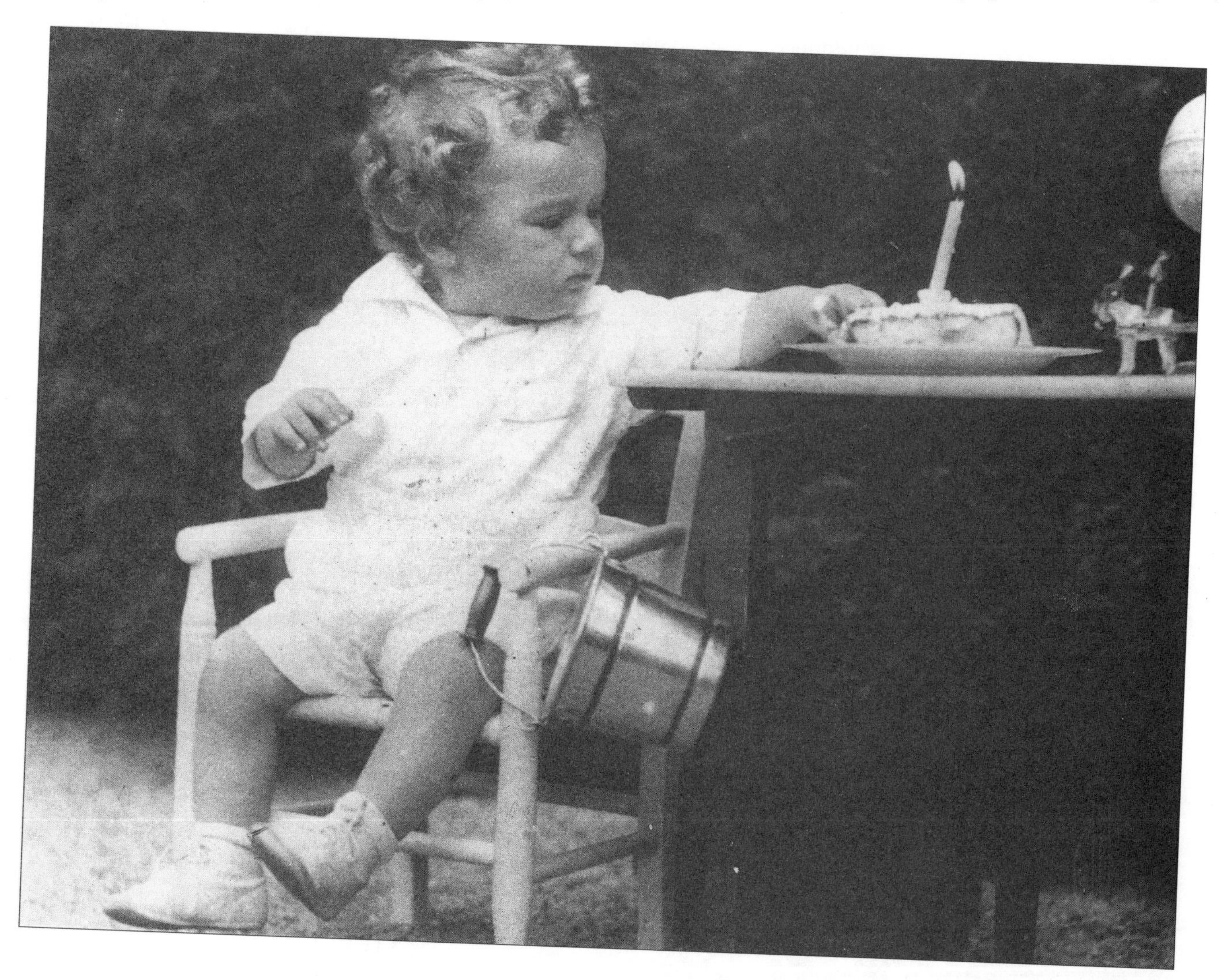

Anne Lindbergh thought that the massive police operation to find the kidnappers might make the criminals afraid to surface. Anne wrote to her mother: 'The detectives are very optimistic although they think it will take time and patience. In fact, they think the kidnappers have gotten themselves into a terrible jam – so much pressure, such a close net all over the country.' She did not think about murder.

'THE DETECTIVES ARE VERY OPTIMISTIC ALTHOUGH THEY THINK IT WILL TAKE TIME AND PATIENCE.'

For two weeks they heard nothing, but then another note was delivered, followed rapidly by several more. The first read: 'We will holt the baby untill everyding is quiet.' The next: 'We are interested to send your Boy back in gud health.' Charles Lindbergh, the aviator with steel nerves, found those same nerves now stretched to breaking point. Concerned about the lack of progress in the police investigation, he went behind the back of the police to negotiate with the kidnappers and one month later paid the ransom through an intermediary called Dr John Condon.

NEITHER LINDBERGH NOR CONDON TRIED TO GRAB THE MYSTERIOUS CHARACTER WHO LED THEM TO THE CEMETARY.

Condon was an eccentric old man who had retired after fifty years teaching, then secured an appointment as a professor at New York's Fordham University. Condon approached Lindbergh and offered himself as the intermediary in negotiations because he had provoked the criminals, and so began to receive the same kind of ransom demands marked with the unique cluster of holes at the bottom of the notes next to a signature. The first note to him, delivered after Condon placed an advertisement in a New York newspaper outlining his proposition to be a negotiator, read: 'Dear Sir: If you are willing to act as go-between in the Lindbergh cace pleace follow stricly instruction.' Lindbergh, at first, was suspicious of Condon, but when he showed him the note with the coded circles at the bottom, he allowed himself to go along with the plan.

Above: ***Charles and Anne Lindbergh in carefree days.***

Condon was given the code-name 'Jafsie' by Lindbergh, who then authorised the old man to place the coded message: 'Mony is Ready, Jafsie' in a New York newspaper. This was in response to a demand for money in the second note the kidnappers sent to Condon. A month later, Condon received another note informing him to read an advertisment in the personal section of the New York Times. That ad told him to go to a New York subway station with the money. At the subway station he found, at the pre-arranged rendezvous spot, a note that read: 'cross the street and follow the fence from the cemetary. direction to 233 street. I will meet you.' In the cemetery, lurking between the gravestones, Condon met a man who told him that the baby was safe. 'Colonel Lindbergh needs some proof,' Condon said, 'before he can hand over the money.' The man said he would send the boy's sleeping suit through the mail within the next day or so. But he said, also, that the ransom demand had been increased to $70,000. Condon replied that it was short notice for such an amount of money. The man seemed to panic then, and asked sharply: 'Have you brought the police?' 'No, you can trust me, I assure you,' replied Condon. Two days later, the baby suit arrived, and was identified by Mrs Lindbergh as the one that little Charles was wearing that fateful night.

MYSTERIOUS MAN CALLED 'JOHN'

Fifty thousand dollars was dropped off by Condon in a subsequent meeting at the cemetry in the Bronx section of New York; and this time, Colonel Lindbergh accompanied Condon, although neither of these two men tried to apprehend or grab the mysterious character who had led them to the cemetery. He called himself 'John' and accepted the box of money handed to him by Condon. He promised to send details of the whereabouts of the child by the next morning's post. This strange encounter was indeed followed by an anonymous letter, marked with the familiar puncture holes.

'The boy is on the Boad Nelly – you will find the Boad between Horseneck Beach and Gay Head near Elizabeth Island.' Lindbergh took 'Boad' to be a misspelling for boat and searched the area near Martha's Vineyard in New England without success. He returned home on 12 May to the dreadful news that the decomposed body of a little boy had been found in a thicket by William Allen, a truck driver, just six miles from his home. The child had died from a severe blow to the skull. The dead baby was identified as Charles Lindbergh, Jnr. The discovery shattered Charles Lindbergh's heart, and the pain of his loss was intensified when he was informed that the baby had died on the night that he was kidnapped.

It was also distressing that the police investigation had not unearthed a single clue as to the identity of the murdering kidnappers. The Lindberghs said that they would have derived some kind of comfort if they knew that the murderer was behind bars, or executed for his crime, but that such wickedness should go unpunished was a hard cross to bear.

As the story gradually disappeared off the front pages, and Charles Lindbergh began to immerse himself in the politics of fascism, at that time gaining popularity in

Above: ***Bruno Hauptmann who, for greed, cruelly kidnapped and killed a small child.***

Left: ***A scene during the hunt for evidence in the first hours after the baby's disappearance.***

Europe, the police continued their dogged, patient detective work. The money paid over by 'Jafsie' was their chief clue, for Lindbergh had been careful to record the serial numbers of the notes he handed over and some of these were readily-convertible gold certificates whose numbers were quickly distributed throughout the country. All banks had been told to be on alert for anyone cashing in certificates that bore the serial numbers of the ones paid out in the Bronx cemetery.

RANSOM CASH DISCOVERED

On 15 September, 1934, a thirty-five-year-old German-born carpenter was arrested after paying for ten gallons of petrol with a $10 gold certificate that carried one of the 'hot' serial numbers – 4U13-41. The quick-thinking petrol pump attendant noted the customer's car registration number and informed police. A quick check on the

Above: ***Charles Lindbergh at Croydon Aerodrome, England, after his courageous flight.***

Right: ***Bruno Hauptmann leans across to address his wife before his murder trial gets underway.***

licence plate of the car revealed that the owner was one Bruno Hauptmann, of 1979 East 222nd Street in the Bronx. When he was arrested several of the ransom certificates were found in his possession. A search of Hauptmann's garage unearthed a further $14,000 of the ransom cash. And a search of his apartment revealed, stencilled behind a cupboard door, the telephone number of go-between Condon.

Hauptmann told his captors that he had come to America in 1923 and that he had been speculating in stocks and shares. 'I have been lucky,' he claimed.'I am not a criminal. Everything I have is my own, not some fruits of a criminal enterprise.' Hauptmann then explained that the bulk of the cash was, in fact, not his, that it was was given to him by a friend called Isidor Fisch, a wealthy fur dealer, to look after until he returned from a trip to Germany. Fisch died in Germany and was never able to corroborate his story.

Above: ***Anne Lindbergh before the dreadful murder of her baby. It was a tragedy from which she never fully recovered.***

Interpol did not exist in those days, but a quick cable to Germany proved that Hauptmann was a liar on at least one point: he was a criminal and in his homeland had been convicted of robbery and managed to escape to America, entering the country illegally under a false name. And further proof was arrayed against him when a taxi-driver identified him as a man who had once asked him to deliver a note to Condon. On 11 October, 1934, Bruno Hauptmann was charged with murder and for attempting to extort money out of Colonel Lindbergh.

HAUPTMANN WAS A CRIMINAL AND IN HIS HOMELAND HAD BEEN CONVICTED OF ROBBERY.

The trial was a sensation when it opened on 2 January, 1935, almost three years after the crime. David Wilentz, the New York State Attorney General,

outlined the prosecution's case to a court packed with pressmen, sketch artists and the curious public. Mrs Lindbergh took the stand and courageously told the events of that tragic night. Colonel Lindbergh rejected assertions from the defence team that members of his staff may have committed the crime. And Betty Gow, who had gone back to her native Scotland, returned to give evidence.

Condon held the court's attention when it was his turn to testify. As the go-between, the man who had handled the negotations between the kidnapper and Lindbergh, his evidence was vital. He said that, after hearing Hauptmann speak, he was convinced that the man he met in the cemetery was, in fact, the accused.

Part of the door jamb of the cupboard, on which Condon's phone number had been scratched, was brought into court. Hauptmann tried to explain it away thus: 'I became interested in the case through reading about it in the newspapers. I jotted it down when Condon's name had been featured, but I did not deliver ransom demands to him.' The evidence continued to mount against Hauptmann. As he sat slumped in the dock, he could hear the cries of the newspaper sellers outside as they hawked the sensational story of the trial. The most damning evidence came from a firm of accountants that had been hired by police to investigate Hauptmann's financial affairs. The accountants calculated that, with his wages and those of his wife Annie's, Hauptmann could only have accrued a capital of just over 6,000 dollars; yet, he had $41,000 although not even his 'speculations' on the stock market had made such profits. The accountants, the police, the Lindberghs and the defence counsel itself were forced to admit that it seemed likely that Hauptmann was holding some of the $35,000 that the Colonel had paid in ransom money for the return of his baby son.

Handwriting experts testified that the accused's writing was the same as that on the ransom notes, and that he was a notori-

Above: ***During the trial, Charles Lindbergh was obliged to read yet again the ill-educated but cruel ransom letters the kidnapper sent to him and his wife.***

Opposite, above: ***The jury who judged John Case. He was charged with obstructing justice in the recovery of the kidnapped baby.***

Opposite, below: ***The accused listens to the evidence mounting against him. The investigation had unearthed detailed and damning proof of his crime, yet Bruno Hauptmann continued to plead his innocence.***

ously bad speller when writing English. One witness said in reference to Hauptmann's spelling: 'He was quite atrocious – simply the worst I have ever come across.'

Finally, police offered up a ladder as the final piece of evidence to link Hauptmann with the crime. A ladder, that was not the Lindbergh's property, had been found at their home after the kidnapping. On closer examination, it proved to be a handmade affair and was designed as three pieces, that could be quickly assembled to form the ladder, but, also, they could be taken apart in seconds to fit neatly in the boot of a car. Such a ladder was perfect equipment for a burglar or a kidnapper. Arthur Koechler appeared before the jury. He was an expert

Right: ***Bruno Hauptmann with his defence attorney, Edward J. Reilly.***

Below: ***Aerial view of the Lindbergh estate in New Jersey from which the baby was taken.***

in wood, and his testimany proved that this ladder had been crafted by the carpenter, Bruno Hauptmann.

Above: ***Bruno Richard Hauptmann is strapped into the electric chair. He was found Guilty and sentenced to death for the murder of baby Lindbergh.***

LADDER WAS THE KEY TO THE CASE

Koechler's testimony became a classic in courtroom evidence, so thorough was both his knowledge of his subject and his investigation into the provenance of the ladder found at the scene of the crime. The author of fifty published works on timber and its uses, Koechler told the court he had examined timbers in Hauptmann's home and could swear on oath that part of the ladder was made from a board lifted from the floor in Hauptmann's attic. Nail holes in the floor corresponded with nail holes in the wood of the ladder, as did the grain of the wood itself. But Koechler was not satisfied with this evidence. He checked and found the sawmill where the wood had been bought. He discovered, too, that Hauptmann once worked at this very sawmill and that he had purchased timber from his employer on 29 Deecember, 1931, three months before the kidnapping.

But despite the overwhelming mass of evidence that proved his guilty involvement in the crime, Bruno Hauptmann continued to plead his innocence. He insisted that everything was circumstantial, that he was spending time with friends at the time that he was supposed to have met Condon and Lindbergh in the cemetery. And he even claimed that the words he misspelled when asked to write them for the police, words that happened to repeat the exact errors of the ransom notes, proved nothing, except that he had been under strain from the long interrogations and abusive treatment meted out by the detectives grilling him. Attorney General Wilentz glared at him during the trial summing up, saying: 'You are a liar and a rather unskillful liar at that.'

'WHY HE CHOSE TO KILL THAT LITTLE BABY BY BASHING HIS HEAD IN, WE'LL NEVER KNOW.'

THE JURY WERE UNANIMOUS IN THEIR VERDICT

The trial lasted until 11 February, 1935, thirty-two days in all, and the transcript of court proceedings filled four thousand pages of closely-typed law books. And the jury, which was out for over eleven hours, were unanimous in their verdict: Guilty. It was Judge Thomas Trenchard's duty to hand down the maximum penalty prescribed under the law. Bruno Hauptmann was to die in the electric chair for his hienous crime.

The prisoner lodged several appeals through the cumbersome American legal system and this delayed his execution. But in the end Bruno Hauptmann, proclaiming his innocence until the end, died at New Jersey's State Jail on 3 April, 1936. His widow Annie is now ninety-three, frail and weak, but she remains convinced that a great miscarriage of justice was done. She still calls repeatedly for a pardon for her husband. She is repeatedly ignored.

Norman Schwarzkopf Senior, whose career took him to police posts in the Middle East and other parts of the world, remained confident that justice had been served. He said: 'Hauptmann was a greedy man who concocted a scheme to get rich quick. Only the scheme he chose is probably one of the most heinous known to man. Why he chose to kill that little baby by bashing his head in, we'll probably never know. It's almost certain that he panicked; men have a peculiar habit of being over-awed by little children. Whatever happened, I for one never doubted his guilt.' And the evidence against Hauptmann was very convincing.

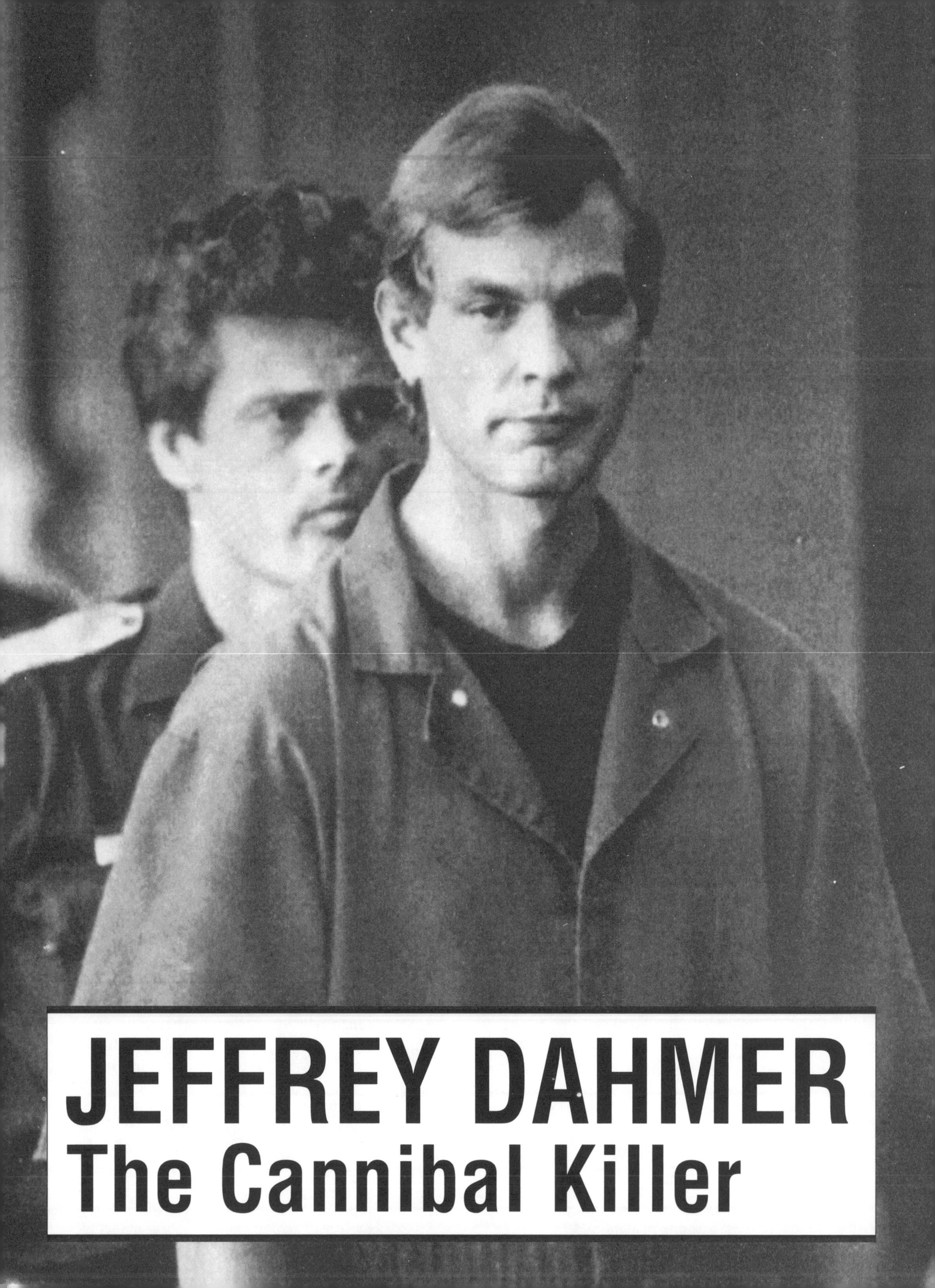

JEFFREY DAHMER
The Cannibal Killer

He seemed to be just another quiet worker at the chocolate factory but there have been few monsters to equal Jeffrey Dahmer – sadist, sodomite, killer and cannibal.

It was a balmy Milwaukee night in July 1991 when horrified police uncovered the secret life of America's most twisted serial killer, Jeffrey Dahmer. His one-bedroomed flat had been turned into a slaughterhouse for his hapless victims and, as the case unfolded, revelations of cannibalism, perverted sex, brutal murder and other unspeakable horrors shocked the whole world.

Photos of police forensic experts carting out vats of acid filled with bones and decomposing body parts, filled television screens around the world and ensured that Milwaukee would forever be known for something other than its beer.

Even though thirty-one year-old Dahmer pleaded Guilty to the murders of fifteen young men he still had to go to trial because he claimed that he was insane – and only a jury could decide whether his acts were the work of a twisted madman or of a cold, calculating, killing machine. The trial itself was one of the most disturbing America had ever witnessed and a national audience of millions of television viewers were to hear tales of human carnage, bizarre sex, sick killings and grisly fantasies that would have ensured a XXX rating had it been a movie.

The strange case of Jeffrey Dahmer ended with a verdict of Guilty and sane. The judge was forced to sentence Dahmer to mandatory, consecutive life terms in prison with no chance of parole for 930 years. The jury disregarded the testimony of psychiatric experts who said that Dahmer was 'psychotic' and suffered from unstoppable sexual urges caused by the mental disease of necrophilia. Dahmer himself appeared to undergo a physical change when he was in prison for the six months before the trial. Expressing remorse and asking to be put to death, the Milwaukee Monster had lost the mad, staring eyes that he had when he was first arrested. But experts still could not agree about his thought processes.

Opposite: ***Jeffrey Dahmer, the man who shocked the world when his depravity was revealed in a criminal court.***

Like the capture of many serial killers, the arrest of Jeffrey Dahmer happened almost by accident. It had been a routine night for Milwaukee police patrolmen Robert Rauth and Rolf Mueller on 22 July 1991 when they spotted a black man running towards their car with a pair of handcuffs dangling from his wrist.

Above: ***Carolyn Smith weeps as court testimony describes the horrible death that her son, Eddie, suffered in the hands of Dahmer.***

HE HAD FLED FOR HIS LIFE

The man with the handcuffs was Tracy Edwards and he told them a wild story about a man in the Oxford Apartments who had threatened to cut out Tracy's heart and eat it. He had fled for his life. It would turn out that Edwards had narrowly avoided becoming victim number eighteen for America's most bizarre and warped serial killer, Jeffrey Dahmer.

THEY SPOTTED A BLACK MAN RUNNING TOWARDS THEIR CAR WITH A PAIR OF HANDCUFFS DANGLING FROM HIS WRISTS.

The two veteran policemen, used to responding to trouble in the rundown section of Milwaukee that had become their beat, took Edwards back to the ordinary looking block of flats and rang the buzzer of one of Dahmer's neighbours. 'Open up, this is the police,' they told John Batchelor through the intercom. He let them in and looked at his watch – it was 11:25pm.

Nothing had prepared the two cops for what they would find after they rapped on the door of apartment number 213 as Tracy Edwards stayed a safe distance away down the corridor. A slight man with dirty-blonde hair and wearing a blue T-shirt and jeans opened the door. As they entered the dingy flat the policemen smelled a foul stench. A hi-tech electronic lock on Dahmer's front door further heightened their suspicions and they started to ask what had been going on. Mueller spotted some pots on top of the stove, some of them filled with a gooey substance and lots of dirty dishes.

Edwards had told the policemen that he had met Dahmer at a downtown shopping mall and agreed to come back to his flat to drink some beer. When he said he wanted to leave Dahmer threatened him with a knife and put the handcuffs on one of his wrists, holding the other end in his hand. When Edwards later recounted his incredibly lucky escape from the Milwaukee Monster to a packed courtroom, he was too frightened to even look across at the defendant. We must assume that Jeffrey Dahmer had wielded a similar dread power over most of his victims.

Above: ***In 1978, Jeffrey Dahmer was normal enough to go to the high school prom with a girl, Bridget Geiger. In 1982, he was photographed by the police when he was arrested for disorderly conduct.(Below)***

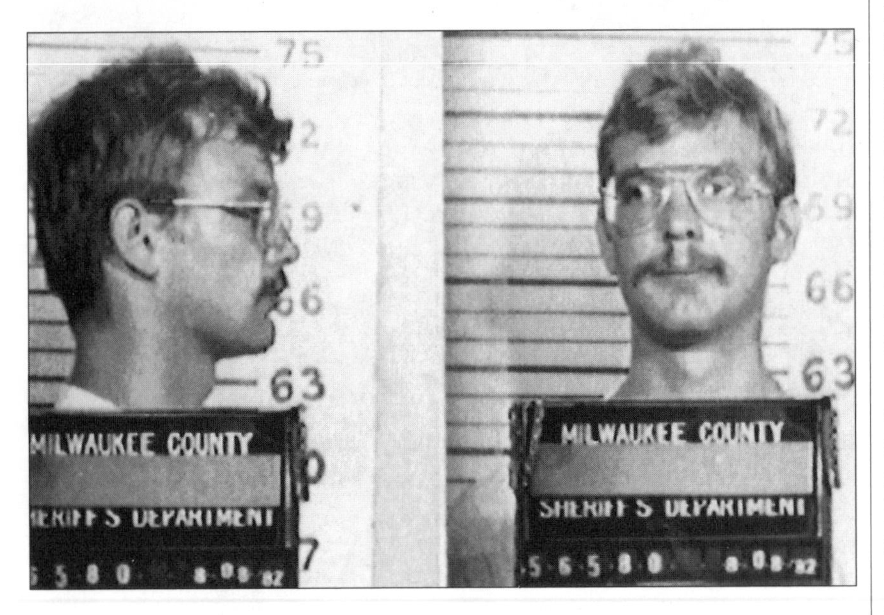

After several hours inside the Dahmer lair, during which time Dahmer lay on top of Edwards' chest and listened to his heart, the killer began to get restless. Edwards testified that Dahmer began going in and out of a trance, chanting and swaying back and forth. This gave Edwards the opportunity to escape. Officer Mueller radioed back to police headquarters to 'run a make' on Dahmer. When they replied that the man was still on probation for a second degree sexual assault charge against a thirteen-year-old boy, the officers instructed Dahmer to lie face down on the floor so they could handcuff him and take him in. It was then that Officer Mueller wandered over to the refigerator and opened it. 'Oh my God! There's a goddamn head in there. He's one sick son of a bitch.'

'OH MY GOD! THERE'S A GODDAMN HEAD IN THERE. HE'S ONE SICK SON OF A BITCH.'

Jeffrey Dahmer had been found out and his killing spree had been brought to an abrupt end, but as the gory details of his murderous orgy began to emerge it became clear that for more than a year, he had been killing people and chopping them up.

A COLLECTION OF POLAROIDS SHOWING DAHMER'S VICTIMS

As forensic specialists began to pour into the apartment building to catalogue the series of horrors, neighbours, awakened by all the commotion, started filing out into the streets. Police found a barrel drum filled with acid and the remains of three human torsos. Decomposed hands and genitals were kept in a lobster pot in one of his cupboards along with human skulls, hands and fingers. A collection of Polaroids was found showing each of Dahmer's fifteen victims in various states of undress and then, according to the forensic report 'in different degrees of surgical excision'. They had been slaughtered, butchered and then dissolved.

Photographs from gay magazines hung on Dahmer's bedroom walls and a collection of pornographic videos, heavy metal records and a tape of 'The Exorcist II' littered the living room. The only normal foodstuffs police found in Dahmer's flat were packets of crisps, a jar of mustard, and some beer. Not only had he been murdering and butchering his prey, he had been eating their flesh as well. He would later tell police how he fried one of his victim's biceps in oil and had it for dinner. In his freezer, police found human hamburgers made up of strips of muscle and flesh. Horrified neighbours watched as police in protective anti-toxic suits carried the evidence out of the building.

Dahmer grew up in a normal American family. His father Lionel worked as a research chemist in Bath, Ohio where he married Joyce Flint in 1959. Jeffrey was born exactly nine months after his parents got married, and doesn't seem to have had a terribly traumatic childhood. His parents divorced when he was eighteen and he was left to fend for himself. He was just about to graduate from the Revere High School and he moved into a motel to be by himself while his mother and father sorted out custody of his eleven-year-old brother. By this time, however, Dahmer was beginning to show signs of being 'a little odd'. He had trouble having relationships with girls, he was considered 'weird' by many of his classmates, and his favourite pastime was imitating mentally retarded people. 'He was a class clown but not in a wholesome sense,' recalled Dave Borsvold. 'He was only amused by the bizarre. He used to trace outlines of bodies out on the floor with chalk. He was definitely a little bit different.' But he did not seem dangerous.

His high school guidance counsellor George Kungle said:'Jeff was never a discipline problem – he was a quiet but not necessarily introverted guy. He never let anyone get to know him well. I would try and talk to him, like you would any kid, hoping to get some insights. He just never said a whole lot about himself.'

'JEFF WAS NEVER A DISCIPLINE PROBLEM – HE WAS A QUIET BUT NOT NECESSARILY INTROVERTED GUY.'

A FATHER'S SENSE OF SHAME

During a bitter divorce Jeffrey's father accused his wife of 'extreme cruelty and gross neglect' and he made references to her 'mental illness' and the medical treatment she was receiving. Even the experts do not know what causes a serial killer to develop, but in Dahmer's case an hereditary mental illness might not be too far from the mark. 'In retrospect I wish I had done more in terms of keeping in touch of what he was doing and visiting him more often,' said Dahmer's father when he discovered what his son had been doing. 'I don't know about feeling guilty for what he did, but I feel guilty that I didn't do more. I feel a deep sense of shame. I think any father who has some sense of responsiblity feels the transfer of shame or the responsibility somehow for this. When I first heard about it I could not associate him with what I was hearing was done. Absolutely not. I didn't think in my wildest dreams he was capable of something like that,' added Dahmer Sr, who paid for an expensive criminal defence lawyer, Gerald Boyle, to act for his son.

'I didn't look at him and see a monster. He acts – under most conditions – polite, kind, courteous. I can only imagine in my mind those occasions when he attacked the victims that was the monster who was out of control.' In Revere High School's yearbook Dahmer is described as a 'very valuable' member of the tennis team. He also played in the school band. In the space reserved for what he would like to do with his life, he said he wanted to attend Ohio State University and then pursue a career in business. It would later emerge that Dahmer had already committed his first murder the year he left school. He often killed and mutilated animals in the woods behind his home, before he killed a young male hitch hiker, Stephen Hicks, who was on his way to a rock concert. Dahmer did indeed go to Ohio State in September of 1978 but he dropped out in January the next year to join the army. Friends who remember him say he was set on the idea of becoming a military policeman.

Above: ***Jeffrey Dahmer, was at last, in 1991, unmasked for the monster he is. Here he is led into court to face charges of murder and cannibalism .***

Instead, Dahmer ended up becoming a medical orderly and was sent to Germany to the Baumholder base in Rhineland-Palatinate state. The army has not revealed why he was discharged before his commission was up, but members of Dahmer's family say it was because of alcoholism. His time in the forces equipped him with a rudimentary knowledge of anatomy. When Dahmer returned to America he started drifting into casual, blue collar jobs that paid little and afforded little respect from anyone. After six months in Miami he moved to Bath, Ohio, where he received a disorderly conduct charge for having an open container of alcohol on the street. In January 1982 he moved to Milwaukee to live with his grandmother, where he dispalyed a pattern of bizarre sexual activity by exposing himself to young children until he was charged with sexual abuse of a thirteen-year-old boy. The young boy's brother was to be a murder victim.

THE YEAR WAS 1988 AND, UNKNOWN TO THE LAW, HE HAD ALREADY KILLED FOUR TIMES...

Right: ***His defence team pleaded insanity on Dahmer's behalf, but the jury were to hear that he had planned his crimes with cunning forethought and in full awareness of his dreadful acts.***

Shortly before he was due to be sentenced for the abuse of the boy, Dahmer wrote a lucid letter to the judge in the case asking for leniency and promising never to do it again. 'The world has enough misery in it without my adding more to it,' he wrote. 'That is why I am requesting a sentence modification. So that I may be allowed to continue my life as a productive member of our society.'

The year was 1988 and, unknown to the law, he had already killed four times. Regardless of his letter Dahmer was sentenced to eight years in jail, though he was released after serving just ten months because he proved to be a model prisoner and was told to report regularly to a probation officer.

FOR ALMOST TWO YEARS THE PROBABTION OFFICER SAT ACROSS A TABLE FROM DAHMER EVERY FIRST TUESDAY OF EACH MONTH. NEVER IN A MILLION YEARS DID SHE DREAM THAT HE COULD BE CAPABLE OF THE BRUTAL BUTCHERY OF THE ELEVEN YOUNG MEN.

For almost two years probation officer Donna Chester sat across a table from Dahmer every first Tuesday of each month for fifteen minutes. Never in a million years did she dream that he could be capable of the brutal butchery of the eleven young men. Thirty-five-year-old Chester, who still works for the Wisconsin State Probation Service, was assigned to Dahmer's case in March 1990 after he was released from prison. To Chester, Jeffrey Dahmer was no different from most of the one hundred and twenty-one criminals that were part of her caseload. He was trying to make his way back into society with the help of counselling and supervision after a bout in jail time that he said he regretted.

As he sat in her room in the district office he would tell Donna how his counselling sessions were going, he would talk about his hobbies, his personal life and the things he did in his spare time. What she did not realise was that this was no ordinary sex offender working his way diligently through rehabilitation. Jeffrey Dahmer held a dark secret close to him. And he was so good at it that Donna even cancelled a home visit to his apartment. A spokesman for the Department of Corrections, Joe Scislowicz, said it was unfair to blame Donna Chester for what happened. He remembered Dahmer as polite, punctual and reliable. 'He was only unable to report on two occasions in two years, otherwise he was here at the same time every month,' said Scislowicz. 'Both times he called ahead and said he wouldn't be able to make it and gave a good reason. He was excused from appearing both times. He was very meticulous about reporting to his probation officer once a month. I'm told he was like that in his work, too.'

NAKED AND BLEEDING, HE RAN FROM DAHMER

Scislowicz would not elaborate on the kind of rehabilitation treatment Dahmer was going through – saying it was a breach of privacy – he said his case file shows that Dahmer felt he was making some progress at working towards his goal of becoming a 'useful contributor to society'. Chester's inability to see through Dahmer's tissue of lies brought criticism from Milwaukee police chief Philip Arreola who spoke out about how the system failed its people and its policemen. 'We try to put these people away for a long time and they get let back out on to the streets,' he said. 'Now we can see the tragic results of a system that has simply ceased to function.'

It was a hard pill for the probation department, and Chester to swallow. They felt they had done all they needed to keep tabs on Dahmer. As Scislowicz said: 'There was a lot of evidence he was doing alright. Most people who have a residence and a good paying job tend to stay out of trouble. This is such an exception, it's not fair to blame it on any individual.'

Arreola got a taste of his own medicine just a few days later when it emerged that a tragic, careless act by three bigotted policemen allowed Dahmer to continue with his killing spree unabated. Choking back tears of embarassment the police chief had to admit that he was bringing in the Internal Affairs Division to investigate reports that three officers actually came face to face with Dahmer on the night of 27 May. One even went inside his flat – and not one of them thought anything was wrong.

The incident involved Konerak Sinthasomphone, a fourteen-year-old Laotian refugee who was seen running out of Dahmer's apartment apparently bleeding. Neighbours, mostly black people, called in the police but were more or less told to 'stop bothering the white guy' according to witnesses. Not only was Sinthasomphone naked and bleeding, but he had been drugged with a heavy dose of sleeping pills – Dahmer's favourite form of rendering his victims unconscious before strangling them – and there were tiny drill marks in his head. Dahmer had fantasised about creating zombie-like lovers that could be his sex slaves and he began to experiment on some of them by doing crude lobotomies with an electric drill and some acid. One poor victim stayed awake for an entire day before finally dying. As soon as the police left the building Dahmer, who told them the boy was his lover, strangled Sinthasomphone, and dismembered his body – all the while taking polaroid pictures. The three policemen responsible have been fired.

Within hours of his arrest Dahmer admitted to killing seventeen people, twelve of them inside his Milwaukee flat and two in a different state. He identified photographs of missing persons for detectives. Forensic psychologists and other experts all testified at his trial, which drew large crowds for three weeks at the Milwaukee County Safety Building. But they could not agree on whether he was able to stop his urge to kill, a crucial aspect of his insanity defence. Dahmer sat emotionless, occasionally stifling yawns, as he listened to detectives and psychiatrists recount hundreds of hours of interviews they conducted with him to trying to understand his vile and terrible acts.

DAHMER HAD FANTASISED ABOUT CREATING ZOMBIE-LIKE LOVERS WHO WOULD BE HIS SEX SLAVES.

Below: ***This young boy, Konarak Sinthaomphona, ran screaming from Dahmer's flat but passing policemen were convinced by Dahmer that he and the boy were playing a 'homosexual game'. They let the boy go. Dahmer killed him***

Below, left: ***Konarak's brother and sister are haunted by their brother's desperate death.***

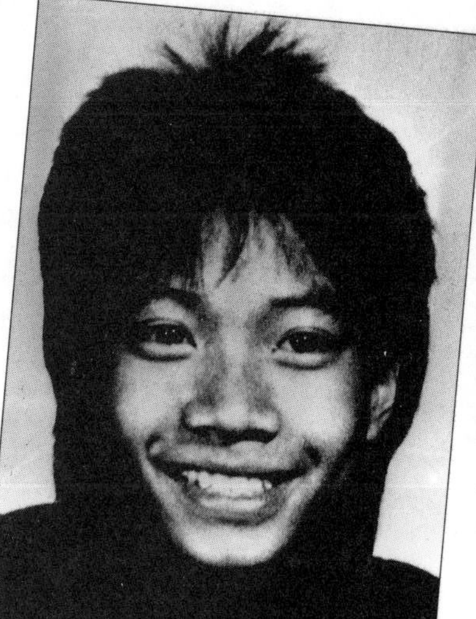

Relatives of his victims, who were almost all black, listened intently to the gruesome testimony. They hugged each other and cried as they heard for the first time what really happened to their loved ones. At the end of the trial, after a jury found that Dahmer was sane, the relatives gave voice to their horror and grief.

For one young woman, seeing Dahmer face to face was too much. Rita Isbell stared into the eyes of the Milwaukee Monster as Judge Laurence Gram invited her to make a statement before sentence was to be imposed. Rita became hysterical when she started talking about her dead brother, Errol Lindsey, who was just nineteen when he was butchered and dismembered by Dahmer in his Milwaukee apartment in 1991. Dahmer had satisfied his twisted fantasies by having sex with the corpse.'I never want to see my mother go through what she went through because of you,' said Isbell. 'Do you understand Jeffrey? Jeffrey, I hate you,' she shouted. Isbell, wearing a sweatshirt that read '100 per cent black', then ran around the outside of the witness box and towards the table where Dahmer was sitting with his lawyers. 'You Mother ****er, I'll kill you Jeffrey,' she screamed hysterically as five court officers held her back.

After other famillies called him 'a devil' and asked the judge to ensure that he never saw daylight again, Dahmer surprised and stunned everyone by asking to make his own statement – an articulate and far reaching apology he had composed himself in his prison cell. Asking for 'no consideration' in his sentencing and declaring that he would have rather had the death penalty – something the state of Wisconsin does not have – Dahmer said: 'It is over now. This has never been a case of trying to get free. I really wanted death for myself. I hope God can forgive me. I know society and the families can never forgive me. I promise to pray every day for their forgiveness. I have seen their tears. If I could give my life right now to bring their loved ones back I would. This was not about hate. I never hated anyone. I knew I was sick or evil or both. Now I have some peace. I know the harm I have caused. I can't undo the terrible harm I have caused but I cooperated as best I could. I am very sorry.

'I understand their rightful hate,' he said of the victims' families, some of whom said they wished he would go to hell. 'I know I will be in prison for the rest of my life. I will turn back to God. I should have stayed with God. I tried and failed and created a holocaust. Only the Lord Jesus Christ can save me from my sins.' Dahmer promised to devote his time behind bars as a study for doctors and psychologists. He said he would to turn himself into a human guinea pig so that they can further examine his bizarre mind to try and find out what would make a human being turn into such a monster. The killer vowed to help psychiatrists to understand what made him do the

Top: ***A Milwaukee policeman is obliged to photograph human bones found in the alley behind Dahmer's apartment.***

Above: ***The freezer where Dahmer kept his nasty store of human flesh.***

ghastly things that he did on his killing, mutilation and cannibalistic spree.

'I pledge to talk to the doctors to help find some answers,' Dahmer said in a prepared statement. 'I know my time in jail will be terrible but I deserve whatever I get because of what I did.' Dahmer – who admitted to detectives that he studied the Satanic scripts – read a passage from the Bible and declared: 'Jesus Christ came to the world to save the sinners, of whom I am the worst.' Dahmer apologised to the victims' families, his probation officer, and even the policemen who were fired. Dahmer also apologised to his father Lionel and step-mother Shari, who both sat quietly and listened intently every day of the court proceedings.

'I regret that the policemen lost their jobs,' said Dahmer. 'I know they did their best. I have hurt my mother, father, step-mother and family. I love them all so much. I only hope they find the same peace I have. I take all the blame for what I did. I hurt many people. I decided to go through with this trial for a number of reasons. I wanted to show these were not hate crimes. I wanted the world to know the truth. I didn't want any unanswered questions. I wanted to find out what it was that caused me to be bad or evil. Perhaps if there are others out there, this all might have helped them.'

ROUND-THE-CLOCK SURVEILLANCE IN ISOLATION

Dahmer was sentenced to a total of one thousand and seventy years in prison on fifteen consecutive counts of murder plus extra sentences for habitual criminality with no possibility of parole for nine hundred and thirty years. Just one day after the sentence he was taken to Wisconsin's toughest jail – the maximum security Columbia Correctional Institution where he is held in a segregated cell. The Portage prison houses five hundred and seventy-five of the worst criminals in the state – sex offenders, murderers, drug dealers and now Jeffrey Dahmer. There is a chance that he could be absorbed into the main prison population but for now he will be under round-the-clock surveillance in isolation. 'At the beginning we will be observing him twenty-four hours a day to ensure that he is not a danger to himself,' said Columbia's warden Jeffrey Endicott. 'The best way for us to do that is to have him in that section of the prison. It is safest for all concerned.'

Endicott added that many inmates are moved out of the isolation block after a few days, but that Dahmer may be kept there longer than others. Many of the one hundred and fifty sex offenders in the prison never leave their single cells or mingle with other prisoners. Fellow serial killer Henry Lee Lucas, who is on death row in a Texas prison said that life in jail for him was 'pure hell'. Lucas, who was convicted of eleven murders and suspected of committing one hundred and forty more, says Dahmer will have a rough time of it. 'He'll be lucky to stay alive in prison. There's a thing in prison about kids, you know,' he said.'If somebody kills a kid like that he'll have a hard way to go.'

Dahmer will have no contact with other prisoners at first and even though he says he no longer wants to kill, guards have been told to take every precaution when dealing with him. All of his food is passed to him through a drawer in a wall to avoid contact and he will be kept under constant surveillance twenty-four hours a day by guards who sit inside a protected 'control bubble'. Columbia Correctional Institution is a large complex, with five watchtowers, razor wire topped high security fences and electronic surveillance of its nineteen-acre perimeter. There is no chance that Dahmer could escape. He is allowed to exercise once a day but is always accompanied by several guards. And he must wear the bright orange jumpsuit uniform he was given when he walked in the front door of the prison.

DAHMER WAS SENTENCED TO A TOTAL OF ONE THOUSAND AND SEVENTY YEARS IN PRISON ON FIFTEEN CONSECUTIVE COUNTS OF MURDER.

Above: ***The freezer, vital evidence to support the charge that Dahmer was a cannibal, is loaded on a police van.***

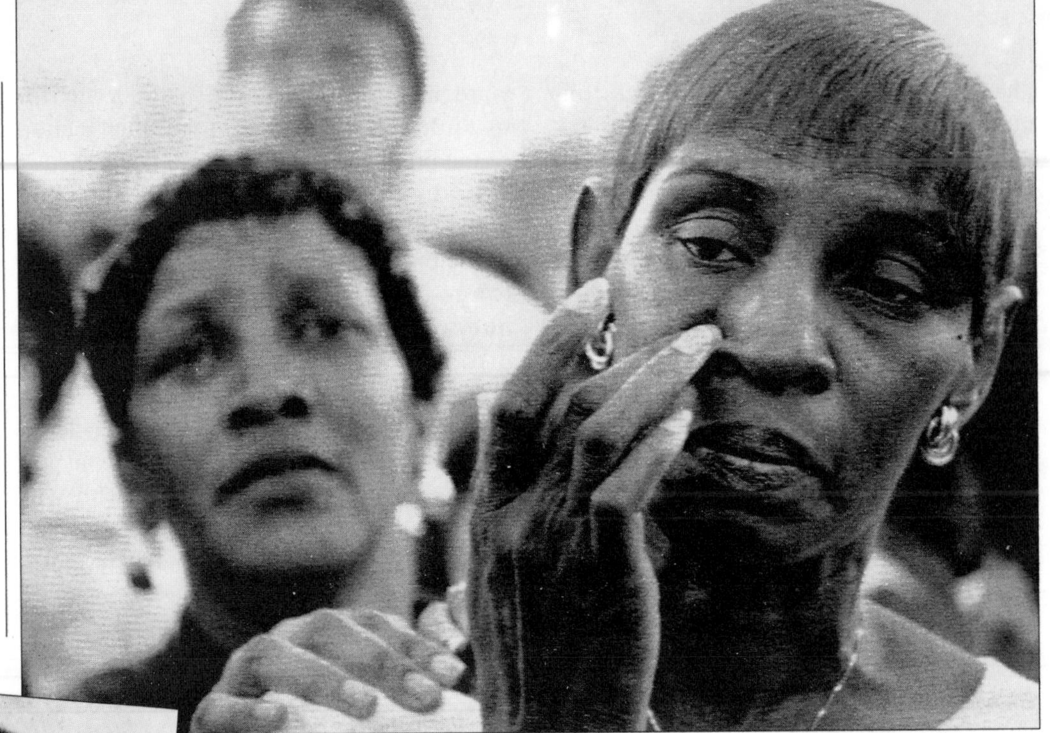

Right: ***Another mother grieves for her son during a candlelit vigil held in Milwaukee for the murdered boys. Her son was Tony Hughes, and he was dismembered by the monster.***

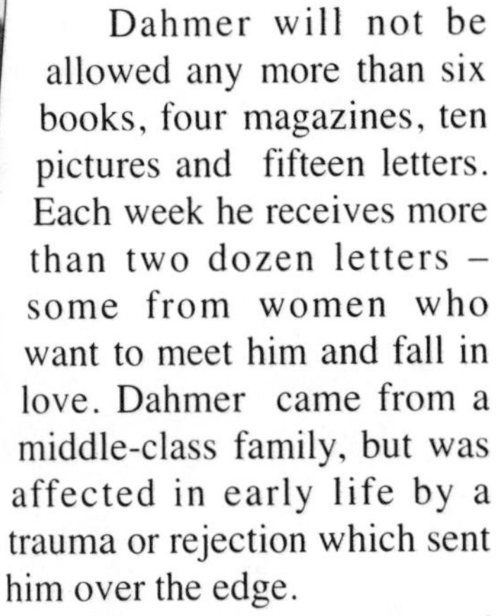

Below: ***Oliver Lacy, one of the many victims. Dahmer decapitated the corpse and kept the head.***

Dahmer will not be allowed any more than six books, four magazines, ten pictures and fifteen letters. Each week he receives more than two dozen letters – some from women who want to meet him and fall in love. Dahmer came from a middle-class family, but was affected in early life by a trauma or rejection which sent him over the edge.

He is similar to many of America's worst mass murderers, in that he can be perfectly normal while he is not in his 'killing mode', and that may work to his advantage in jail. Ed Gein was working as a babysitter while he was spending his nights digging up graves; Ted Bundy worked at a Samaritans' hotline in Seattle in between killings; John Wayne Gacy performed as a clown at childrens' parties; amd David Berkowitz now spends much of his time counselling other inmates at a New York state high security prison.

He helps them with their problems, reads their mail to them and cleans floors. He is considered a model prisoner and will be elligible for parole in ten years. 'Many of these killers are frequently glib and superficially charming, helpful, sweet and kind,' said Helen Morrison, a Chicago psychiatrist and serial killer expert. 'I'm sure Dahmer falls into that same category.' Judith Becker, who testified at the Dahmer trial for the defence, says it is too soon to tell how the prison term will affect Dahmer's personality or his mind. 'He did indicate to me that he hated what he had been doing and he talked about a 'nuclear explosion' that had happened within him since he had been caught,' she said. 'He's talked about killing himself, but obviously he won't be able to do that in prison. He says he is sorry for what he did and that he feels pain for the relatives of the victims. He has already had a lot of time on his own to think about that, and he seems to be coping with it now. The fantasies have stopped, he says. But there is no way of really knowing if they will start up again.'

THE CHANCES ARE THAT HE COULD BECOME A MODEL PRISONER

'The prosecution made a strong case by identifying that Dahmer was able to make definite decisions not to do things at certain times,' said David Barlow, an assistant professor of criminal justice at the University of Wisconsin. Richard Kling, who defended serial killer John Wayne Gacy, added: 'I don't think there is a person in the world who would come in and say Dahmer isn't abnormal. The problem is that abnormal doesn't add up to insanity.' How he deals with being in prison is something that will fascinate

HE IS SIMILAR TO MANY OF AMERICA'S WORST MASS MURDERERS IN THAT HE CAN BE PERFECTLY NORMAL WHILE HE IS NOT IN HIS 'KILLING MODE'.

psychiatric experts for years to come. The chances are that he could become a model prisoner, with the ability to be outwardly friendly to both fellow inmates and guards.

During the trial McCann pointed out Dahmer's ability to manipulate doctors and psychiatrists for his own ends. His supply of prescription sleeping pills – which he used for drugging his victims before he strangled them – came from doctors who thought he was having trouble sleeping.

Dahmer also deliberately misled court appointed therapists who were trying to help him after he was convicted of sexual assault. He rejected the hand that could have helped him,' said McCann. 'He knew what he was doing.' No matter what happens the files of Jeffrey Dahmer will provide endless hours of research material for the FBI's academy in Quantico, Virginia – where special agents are trained to produce profiles of serial killers. Although the project is temporarily dormant after the departure of its director, Robert Ressler, Dahmer's court files will be entered into the FBI's extensive databanks on serial killers.

'SILENCE OF THE LAMBS'

Ressler, who has interviewed such killers as Charles Manson, Sirhan Sirhan, Ted Bundy, John Wayne Gacy, and 'Son of Sam' killer David Berkowitz will attempt to see Dahmer so that he can include his files in his rogue's gallery.'How can a person be sane and do these horrendous acts ?'. He would be a fascinating study for me,' said Ressler, who now runs his own investigating company. 'Any information we can collect on individuals like Dahmer is like gold dust in tracking down others out there who might be doing the same thing.'

In the film 'Silence of the Lambs' Jodie Foster played a young FBI agent who had to befriend the demented Hopkins character – Hannibal the Cannibal – so that she could help catch another serial killer, a murderer based on Wisconsin's other famous maniac, Ed Gein. Gein killed women and then skinned them to satisfy his twisted transvestite fantasies. He also dug up freshly buried bodies so that he could use their skin to build himself a body. He was found mentally incompetent to stand trial in 1957 and so never had the opportunity to plead guilty. He died at the Mendota Mental Health Institute in Madison in 1984. Other psychiatric experts have pointed out that a thorough investigation of Dahmer would be invaluable as research material into sexual perversion.

DAHMER DELIBERATELY MISLED COURT-APPOINTED THERAPISTS WHO WERE TRYING TO HELP HIM AFTER HE WAS CONVICTED OF SEXUAL ASSAULT.

Judith Becker said: 'We could learn a tremendous amount from studying Dahmer because necrophiliacs are extremely rare. I have not seen anywhere in the literature the sucessful treatment of this disorder.' Even the most highly qualified experts cannot agree on what kind of demons live inside the mind of Jeffrey Dahmer. He showed early on in his life a twisted fascination with the macabre and the bizarre. Some psychiatrists claim that the emotional distance between him and his parents might have contributed to his feelings of abandonment. Those feelings fuelled his ghastly killing spree – he told doctors that he killed his victims because he didn't want them to leave him. Some experts say being locked up for life with other criminals who won't be leaving might actually appeal to the perverse needs of Jeffrey Dahmer.

Above: ***Jeffrey Dahmer claimed to feel 'remorse' for his acts. But it needed a police investigation to provoke these feelings in him.***

'One great myth about serial killers is that they secretly want to get caught,' said James Fox, a professor of criminal justice

SOUVENIRS ARE VERY IMPORTANT TO THE DISORGANISED SERIAL KILLERS BECAUSE THEY REMIND THEM OF THE BEST TIMES THEY HAD. DAHMER'S MURDERS WERE DRIVEN BY HIS FANTASIES OF DESTRUCTION, TIED UP WITH A SEXUAL DESIRE.'

at Boston's Northeastern University and author of 'Mass Murder: The Growing Menace'. 'That's just not true, these guys enjoy what they do. They might get a little guilty afterwards for a while, but the fantasies that drive them are so powerful that they have to do it again soon. Dahmer will not be able to do it again now that he's in jail and I'm sure he won't be happy about that. He doesn't even have any of his souvenirs – the photos or even the body parts – to look at anymore. That may be why he has asked for the death penalty, he has nothing else to live for. Souvenirs are very important to the disorganised serial killers because they remind them of the best times they had. Dahmer's murders were driven by his fantasies of destruction, tied up with a sexual desire.'

Prosecutor E. Michael McCann said that Dahmer has always managed to control his violent tendencies when he has been in closely controlled situations and some feel that prison life will do him a lot of good.

DAHMER LONGS FOR DEATH

Worst of all for Dahmer will be the long hours of contemplation he will have to spend alone. He told detectives after his arrest that he wished Wisconsin or Ohio had the death penalty. Now he will have to spend the next forty years thinking about what he did. 'It will probably tear him apart,' said one expert. 'If the court didn't think he was insane when he killed, just wait a few years and see what the torture of his acts does to his mind.'

Dahmer may have to go through the trial process all over again in Ohio where he killed his first victim in 1978. But Ohio, like Wisconsin, has no death penalty – the one thing that Dahmer has wished for.

The world will be a safer place without Jeffrey Dahmer. But the world might never know what it was that drove him to commit some of the worst crimes in American history. One thing is certain, inmates at Columbia will not be jumping over each other for a chance to share a cell with him.

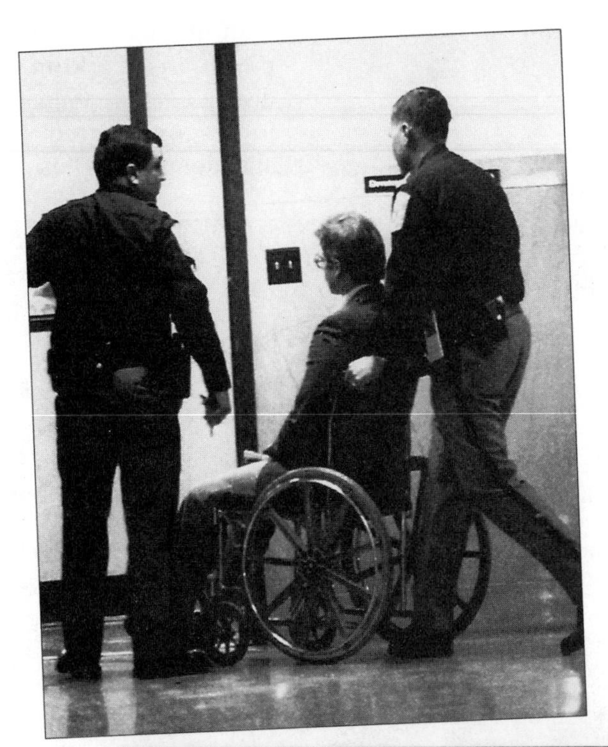

Above: ***The Milwaukee Monster is wheeled into court. His hands and legs were shackled in irons as befits a dangerous beast.***

Right: ***Lionel and Shane Dahmer, Jeffrey's father and stepmother, sat in court throughout his trial.***

VICTIMS AS NAMED BY PROSECUTOR'S OFFICE:

1 January 1988 – James Doxtator
Killed at age fifteen at Dahmer's grandmother's house. Strangled after drinking sleeping potion. Dismembered, bones smashed with a sledgehammer.
2 March 1988 – Richard Guerrero
Killed at age twenty-three at grandmother's house. Drugged him and then dismembered the body.
3 March 1989 – Anthony Sears
Killed at age twenty-four at grandmother's house. Strangled and dismembered. Dahmer kept his skull, boiled off the skin and then painted the skull as a souvenir.
4 May 1990 – Raymond Smith, aka Ricky Beeks
Killed at age thirty in Apartment 213. Strangled after being drugged. Dahmer had sex with the dead body. Dismembered him but kept the skull and painted it.
5 July 1990 – Edward Smith
Killed at age twenty-eight. Dismembered and disposed of in rubbish bags.
6 September 1990 – Ernest Miller
Killed at age twenty-three. Dahmer slit his throat, dismembered him and kept his biceps in the freezer to eat later. Also kept the skull and skeleton which he bleached.
7 October 1990 – David Thomas
Killed at age twenty-three. Killed even though he was not Dahmer's 'type' for fear that he would tell police he had been drugged. Body disposed of.
8 February 1991 – Curtis Straughter
Killed at age seventeen. Strangled with a strap after being drugged. Dismembered him but kept the skull.
9 April 1991 – Errol Lindsey
Killed at age nineteen. Strangled him and then had sex. Dismembered the body and kept the skull.
10 May 1991 – Anthony Hughes
Killed at age thirty-two. Strangled and dismembered him but kept the skull.
11 May 1991 – Konerak Sinthasomphone
Killed at age fifteen. Murdered after police left Dahmer's apartment following telephone call from neighbours. Strangled, dismembered but kept the skull.
12 June 1991 – Matt Turner aka Donald Montrell
Killed at age twenty-one. Strangled with a strap. Kept his head in the freezer and put his body in the acid-filled barrel.
13 July 1991 – Jeremiah Weinberger
Killed at age twenty-four. Strangled with his hands. Put his head in the freezer and his body in the barrel.
14 July 1991 – Oliver Lacy
Killed at age twenty-five. Strangled him and then had sex. Placed head in the bottom of the fridge and kept his heart in the freezer to eat later. Also kept his body in the freezer.
15 July 1991 – Joseph Bradehoft
Killed at age twenty-five. Strangled with a strap while he slept. Dismembered, head put in the freezer and body in the barrel.

Two additional victims Dahmer has admitted killing were not in the Milwaukee charges. They were:

Stephen Hicks was killed in Dahmer's parents' home in Bath, Ohio. Dahmer killed him with a barbell, then disposed of the body in the woods.

Stephen Tuomi killed in Milwaukee hotel room in September 1987. Dahmer says he doesn't remember how he killed the man, but he took his body back to his grandmother's house in a trunk and dismembered him.

Above: ***Investigators were sent to Dahmer's boyhood home to look for the remains of the Monster's first victim, killed in 1978.***

HE DOESN'T REMEMBER HOW HE KILLED, BUT HE TOOK THE BODY BACK TO HIS GRANDMOTHER'S HOUSE AND DISMEMBERED IT.

GRAHAM YOUNG
The Broadmoor Poisoner

Is it possible for a child to be born evil? Graham Young was a prodigy in poison, experimenting with deadly potions even before he was sixteen. And he killed his family and friends as if they were laboratory rats.

Even as a small child, Graham Young was entranced by poisons. Other people may regard such substances with alarm and caution but Graham played with them, learnt their various deadly properties and longed to use them.

Like Ian Brady, the infamous Moors Murderer, Graham Young had a lonely childhood, and in his sullen resentment of the world, turned to other outsiders in his search for role models. Dr Crippen, the wife murderer, was an idol, as was the Victorian poisoner, William Palmer. In contemplating their lives and dreadful acts, Graham Young found a kind of solace which he never got from his family.

He was born in September 1947, and his mother died when he was just three months old. He was cared for by his father's sister, Auntie Winifred, and her husband, Uncle Jack and their's was an affectionate household. But at the age of two his life changed when he was sent to live with his father, who had married a twenty-six-year-old woman called Molly. Psychologists would later say that 'the terrible coldness' that characterised Young was formed by the truama of separation from his first home. He never trusted any affection after that, believing only that it would end in pain and rejection.

Relations with his stepmother were cordial but she never lavished on him the brand of intense loving he craved. Perhaps she found it difficult, for Graham was rummaging through the chemist's rubbish bins in his search for poisons, and was reading books on Satanism by the time he was nine years old. He began wearing a swastika badge that he found at a jumble sale and refused to take it off, even for his teachers at school. Yet Graham was an exceptionally intelligent child, with a strong scientific ability. To celebrate his achievement in passing the eleven-plus examination, his father gave the boy his first chemistry set.

Opposite: ***The child prodigy in poison, Graham Young, is led into custody.***

Below: ***David Tilson, a victim who survived the poisons.***

This gift was the key to the wonderful world of poisons that Graham longed to master. The phials and bunsen burners, the laboratory pipettes and crucibles became his toys at an age when most boys have their pockets stuffed with conkers and fudge. His private games were also more sinister than those of the normal child. Graham liked to witness the death throes of the mice that he fed with the poisons he brewed from his chemistry set. When his stepmother angrily removed a live mouse, and demanded that he stop bringing them into the house, he drew a picture of a craggy tombstone toppling over a mound, inscribed with the words: 'In Hateful Memory of Molly Young, R.I.P.' Graham made sure that the poor woman saw this nasty little drawing.

HE NEVER TRUSTED ANY AFFECTION, BELIEVING ONLY THAT IT WOULD END IN PAIN AND REJECTION.

The youngster took to stealing chemicals from his school and he took to carrying a bottle of ether from which he would frequently take sniffs; he raided his stepmother's cosmetics cabinet to get at nail polish remover, which he used to kill a frog in one of his experiments in the effects of poison. By the time he was twelve, his teachers at the John Kelly Secondary School in Willesden knew that Graham had an unusual expertise, not only in poisons, but in his general pharmaceutical knowledge. The child knew the ingredients

of most household medicines, and was able to diagnose minor illnesses.

But medicine and its life-saving properties were not of real interest to the child boffin. He preferred poisons and their deadly effects. When he was thirteen, Graham found a book that would forever change his life. It was the story of the nineteenth-century poisoner Dr Edward Pritchard, who killed his wife and his mother with the poison antimony. Antimony, a slow working toxin, causes cramps, nausea and swellings in the victim. These symptoms have often led to an incorrect diagnoses from doctors, and this fact has, naturally, made the poison a favourite among murderers.

CHRIS HAD TO BE PUNISHED. GRAHAM BEGAN TO LACE HIS FRIEND'S SANDWICHES WITH ANTIMONY AND WATCHED THE RESULTS WITH SATISFACTION.

Left: ***Graham Young was incarcerated in hospitals and prisons, but he still managed to experiment with his poisons.***

Opposite, above: ***The poisoner, whose youth and ruthlessness horrified the nation, was obscured by a blanket as he was bundled into a police van.***

Opposite, below: ***The sweet face of a boy but the Young family were not entirley fooled. They knew something was wrong with the child, Graham.***

MRS YOUNG SUFFERED SEVERE VOMITING ATTACKS. THEN GRAHAM'S FATHER EXPERIENCED SIMILAR SYMPTOMS, AS DID HIS AUNTIE WINIFRED.

Chemist Geoffrey Reis in High Street, Neasden, sold Graham Young the poison antimony. The boy lied about his age and claimed he was seventeen. Reis explained to the police that the boy's knowledge of poisons was so vast, and he outlined in such detail the chemical experiments in which he intended to use the restricted merchandise, that the chemist naturally assumed him to be older than a mere thirteen-year-old. And neither was Graham Young strictly truthful in describing his experiments to the chemist.

Chris Williams was one of Graham's few schoolboy friends who shared his love of chemistry. He had even invited Chris to his bedroom laboratory to share the pleasure of watching mice die in agony. But Chris Williams began hanging around with another boy, and Graham interpreted this as a persoanl rejection. Chris had to be punished. Graham began to lace his friend's sandwiches with antimony and watched the results with satisfaction. After Chris had suffered two violent vomiting attacks, his family sent him to a specialist who was unable to diagnose the problem. Throughout the early part of 1961, Graham continued to administer doses of poison to his school chum.

EPIDEMIC OF POISONING

Young took to carrying a phial of antimony around with him all the time, calling it 'my little friend'. But his stepmother found the bottle, marked with a skull and crossbones, and put a stop to her stepson's shopping trips when she herself informed the chemist, Mr Reis, of Graham's age. Thwarted but by no means defeated, Graham switched to a new supplier, and a new target. Molly Young would be punished for this.

In October and November, 1961, Mrs Young suffered severe vomiting attacks. Then Graham's father experienced similar symptoms, as did his Auntie Winifred. On one occasion, Graham spiked his own food in error, and he, too, was violently ill, but this did not deter the young poisoner. Using antimony tartrate which he bought from Edgar Davies – another chemist similarly fooled by his advanced knowledge of poisons – he moved on to his step-sister. The girl tasted something odd, and spat out her tea, accusing her mother of leaving some washing-up liquid in the cup.

Winifred was the first to be diagnosed as a poison victim when she had to be helped from a London Underground train on her way to work one morning, in the summer of 1962. Dizzy, her eyes blinded with pain and feeling very ill, she was rushed by ambulance to the Middlesex Hospital where a doctor said she was suffering from belladonna poisoning, the toxin released from the berries of the deadly nightshade weed. Winifred believed that her nephew was to blame, but a search of his room failed to give evidence to her fears. Molly Young's health continued to decline as Graham fed her increasing doses of the antimony tartrate. Early in 1962 she died. At the age of fourteen, Graham Young had committed the perfect murder. He was arrested on suspicion of causing his stepmother's death, but he was released without charge. Molly was cremated and the evidence, the poison in her bloodstream, went with her.

HIS FATHER WAS INFORMED THAT HE WAS LUCKY TO BE ALIVE, BUT THAT HIS LIVER WAS PERMANENTLY DAMAGED.

Graham Young was now assured of his powers to punish those who annoyed or rejected him. Besides, he still had some unfinished business. Dad was to be fed further doses of antimony, as was his unfortunate schoolfriend who continued to suffer violent attacks of nausea, but was still alive. Fred Young collapsed and was rushed to Willesden Hospital where doctors diagnosed arsenic poisoning. 'How ridiculous!' sneered Graham when he visited his father in hospital. 'Fancy not knowing how to tell the difference between antimony and arsenic poisoning!' He explained to the doctors that his father showed all the symptoms of antimony poisoning, but offered no explanation as to how the poison entered his father's system. His father was informed that he was lucky to be alive, but that his liver was permanently damaged. He was allowed home, but was back in hospital within a couple of days because Graham could not resist giving his father another dose in his morning tea.

The Young family were, by now, thoroughly alarmed by their suspicions that their own Graham might be causing their various illnesses. They did not like the way Graham seemed to brighten up and become keenly interested whenever he was discussing the finer points of poison with hospital staff. His father told Aunt Winifred to keep an eye on him, but it was to be his chemistry master at school who spotted the boy's toxic ways. The teacher went through Graham's desk at school, discovering notebooks with lurid pictures of men in their death throes, empty bottles of poison by their sides. He discovered phials of antimony tartrate alongside the drawings, plus detailed notes of what doseages of particular poisons are needed to kill an adult human being. After voicing his concerns to the school headmaster, the two teachers decided to inform the police. The police, in turn, decided to get a psychiatrist to help them trap Graham.

Posing as a careers guidance officer, the psychiatrist interviewed the boy, asking him what he would like to do when he left

school. The doctor was both astounded and horrified at the detailed knowledge the boy had about poisons and their effects. One by one Graham reeled them off, leaving no doubt whatsoever in the psychiatrist's mind that this boy was a psycopath. His report prompted the police to search Young's room. This revealed seven different types of poison stashed in various hiding places, and included a copious amount of antimony tartrate.

Graham Young encountered the police when he came home from school. He reeked of the ether he habitually sniffed, and vehemently denied any involvement in the poisoning of his family. But Young's vanity overcame him. As he liked to brag to the doctors and the psychiatrist, showing off his knowledge of poison, so he could not resist telling the police that he was a successful poisoner. He confessed all, listing the doseages, the times and the methods he used to dispense the poison.

Left: ***Jethro Batt whose evidence helped convict the mad poisoner.***

Below: ***John Williams who told the court of Young's repeated attempts to kill him with poison.***

At Ashford Remand Centre he was subjected to a battery of psychiatric and psychological testing. The doctors who examined him recognised that his was a rare problem, for Young was incapable of comprehending his guilt. 'He has a distinct lack of moral sense, an idea that he is neither bound to nor governed by the rules which apply to other members in society,' was the official verdict. Indeed, Young relished telling the doctors, who were probing his warped emotional state, about his potions and how he loved his father, but that he came to view his parent as a guinea pig for experiments in poison. He told them: 'I chose my family because they were close at hand, where I could observe and note the results of my experiments.' There was no remorse, however. 'I love my antimony,' he explained. 'I love the power it gives me.'

The case of the schoolboy poisoner captured the public imagination when he came before the stern judge Mr Justice

Melford Stevenson on 6 July, 1962, at the Old Bailey. This is Britain's highest court, where half-a-century before, Graham's hero Dr Crippen, had been condemned to death.

Graham Young was charged with poisoning his father, his aunt and his school chum. He spoke only once at his trial, to plead guilty to the charges, but a statement that he made while in custody was read out. Graham told the police: 'I knew that the doses I was giving were not fatal, but I knew I was doing wrong. It grew on me like a drug habit, except it was not me who was taking the drugs. I realised how stupid I have been with these poisons. I knew this all along but I could not stop it.'

A psychiatrist, after testifying that Young was suffering from a psychopathic disorder, recommended the accused be incarcerated in Broadmoor, Britain's top security mental hospital. The judge asked whether a grim, forbidding place such as Broadmoor was the right institution for such a young boy, but after further testimony from Dr Donald Blair, a psychiatrist who had also examined Young, he – the judge – was left with little choice. Blair told the court: 'There is no doubt in my mind that this youth is, at present, a very serious danger to other people. His intense obsession and almost exclusive interest in drugs and their poisoning effect is not likely to change, and he could well repeat his cool, calm, calculating administration of these poisons at any time.'

Young was sent to Broadmoor with an instruction that he should not be released without the permission of the Home Secretary. It was not, however, the last that the world would hear of Graham Young and his potions.

POISONER BEHIND BARS

Far from being an unsuitable place for Graham, Broadmoor was actually a home-from-home for him. The institute is a hospital, after all, and the young poisoner was surrounded by all the medicines and drugs and poisons that he could wish for. He enjoyed lecturing the staff on toxins, and often gave advice to nurses on drugs when no doctors were on hand. Suspicion, however, fell upon him when a fellow inmate, twenty-three-year-old double-murderer John Berridge, died of cyanide poisoning. But Graham was never charged with his murder, although he spent many hours explaining to other inmates how the poison could be extracted from the leaves of the laurel bushes which grew in the hospital grounds.

Young's room in Broadmoor became a shrine to Nazism, heavily decorated with swastikas. He even grew a toothbrush moustache and combed his hair in a fashion that imitated that of Adolf Hitler. He managed to secure a 'green card' – the special pass allowing him to freely roam the hospital wards and gardens. The pass was issued by the psychiatric staff in contradiction to the wishes and advice of the day-to-day nursing staff. The card gave Young the opportunity to collect leaves and plants that contained poisonous materials, and to steal chemicals. The nursing staff often found jars of poison, not on the shelves where they were supposed to be, but in odd places.Young owned up to hiding some of these, but not all. Inexplicable outbreaks of stomach aches and cramps were endured by both staff and

Above: ***Winifred Young, Graham's sister, and his aunt who listened intently to the court evidence against him.***

'THERE IS NO DOUBT IN MY MIND THAT THIS YOUTH IS, AT PRESENT, A VERY SERIOUS DANGER TO OTHER PEOPLE.'

patients; hindsight dictates that Young had been busy dispensing his potions freely-round the large prison hospital.

With the support of two senior doctors who did not want to see him institutionalised for the rest of his life, Graham was able to convince the parole board to free him for Christmas in 1970. He spent it with his Auntie Win, but his return to Broadmoor after the holidays made him more resentful than ever. He wrote a note that nursing staff found, saying: 'When I get out of here I intend to kill one person for every year I have spent inside.'

Nursing staff say they heard him boasting, when he thought no staff were listening, how he wanted to be the most infamous poisoner since Crippen. And the note he wrote remained on their files. Yet Graham Young was released after nine years. At the age of twenty-three he returned to his forgiving Auntie Winifred at her home in Hemel Hempstead, Hertfordshire, before moving on to a hostel in Chippenham where he began his new life.

ANOTHER FRIEND POISONED

Within weeks he was up to his old tricks again. A keen amateur footballer called Trevor Sparkes, who was with Young at a training centre, suffered cramps and pain over a six-month period, and was so debilitated by the mysterious 'illness' that he would never play football again. Sparkes would testify that he and Young enjoyed a friendship, and it never occurred to the footballer that he was being systematically poisoned by his friend.

Above: ***Broadmoor, the mental hospital where Young was confined.***
Below: ***Frederick Young, the father who nearly died.***

In April, 1971, Graham saw an advertisement, offering employment for a storeman with the John Hadland Company of Bovingdon, in Hertfordshire. Hadland's was a well-established family firm that manufactured high grade optical and photographic equipment. Graham impressed Managing Director, Godfrey Foster, at the interview, and explained that his long break from regular employment was due to a nervous breakdown. Foster checked up with the training centre and also Broadmoor, and he received such glowing references as to the young man's abilities and recovery that he offered him the job without hesitation..

On Monday 10 May, 1971, Graham Young arrived at Hadlands. The company thought they were getting a storeman. In reality, they had hired an angel of death. Young rented a bedsitter, and the cupboards and shelves were soon filled with a collec-

tion of poisons. At work he was regarded as a quiet, remote young man unless the conversation turned to politics or chemistry when he became belligerent and articulate. His best friend at work was forty-one-year-

Below: ***Frederick Young, Graham's father and the long-suffering Aunt Winnie. Graham tried to poison both of them.***

old Ron Hewitt whose job he was taking. Ron stayed on to show the new man the ropes and introduced him to the other hands in the plant. Many showed great kindness to Young, lending him money and giving him cigarettes when he had none. Young repaid their warmth by rushing to serve them from the morning tea trolley.

On Thursday 3 June, less than a month after Graham started work, Bob Egle, fifty-nine, who worked as storeroom boss, was taken ill with diarrhoea, cramps and nausea. Next, Ron Hewitt fell violently ill, suffering the same symptoms but with burning sensations at the back of his throat. Workers at Hadlands called the mystery pains 'the bug'. In fact, the symptoms were caused by doses of Thallium, an extremely toxic poison. Young bought the poison from chemists in London, and then laced his workmates' tea with the deadly, but tasteless and odourless chemical. On Wednesday, 7 July, Bob Egle died. His was a horrible, painful death, yet there was no inquest on his body because doctors diagnosed his illness as bronchial-pneumonia linked to polyneuritis.

In September, after a relatively pain-free summer for the staff at Hadlands, because Young was often absent from work, Fred Biggs, a part-time worker, died after suffering agonising cramps and pains over a twenty-day period. Young feigned sympathy for him, as he had for his other victims. 'Poor old Fred,' he said to colleague, Diana Smart. 'It's terrible. I wonder what went wrong with him. I was very fond of Fred.' Four other workers fell victim to awful illnesses, two of them losing all their hair, followed by severe cases of depression.

The company became so concerned by the poor health of their workforce, that they called in a local doctor, Iain Anderson, to check the employees, but he was unable to determine the source of the 'bug'. But then Anderson talked to Graham Young, who unable to suppress his vanity, reeled off mind-numbing statistics about poisons and their effects and Anderson's amazement turned to suspicion. He consulted the company management, who called Scotland Yard. The police ran a background check on

IT WAS A RELATIVELY PAIN-FREE SUMMER FOR THE STAFF AT HADLANDS BECAUSE YOUNG WAS OFTEN ABSENT FROM WORK.

FOUR OTHER WORKERS FELL VICTIM TO AWFUL ILLNESSES, TWO OF THEM LOSING ALL THEIR HAIR, FOLLOWED BY SEVERE CASES OF DEPRESSION.

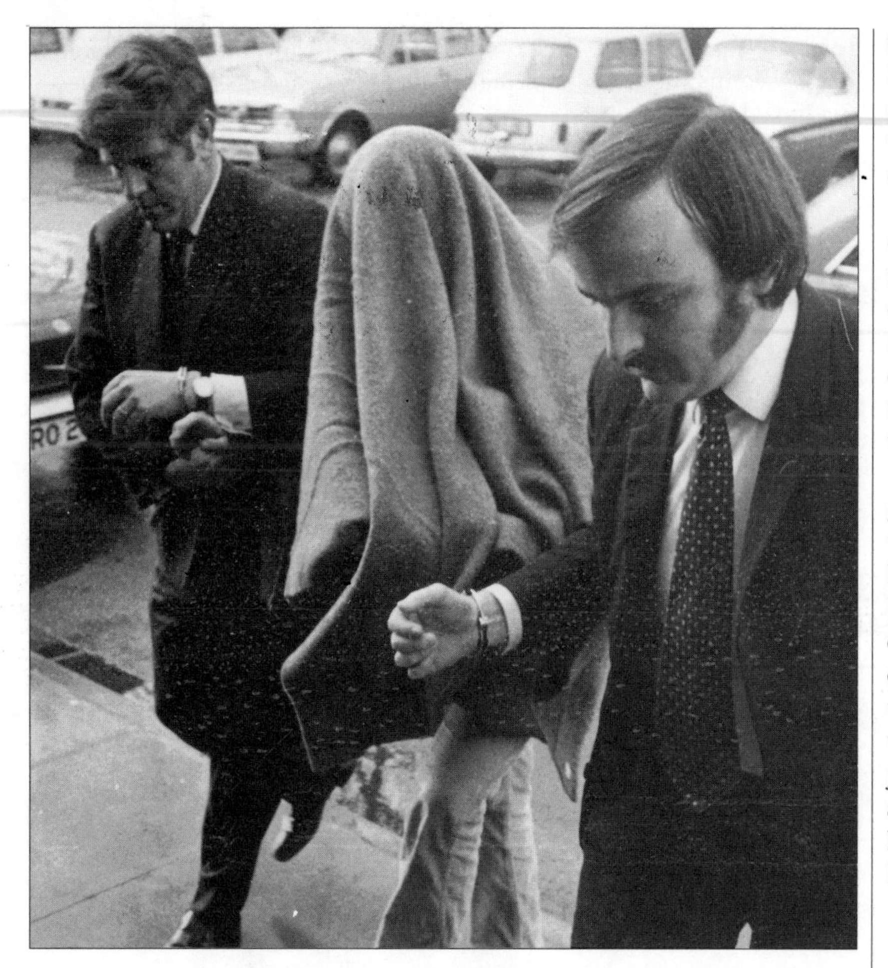

Above: ***Graham Young taken into court by law officers. He was given a long sentence, but died in prison – not of self-administered poison, but a heart attack.***

all company employees, while forensic scientists from the government research station at Aldermaston were asked to analyse samples taken from the poorly members of staff. The scientists proved that Thallium had caused the deaths and the illnesses among the staff at Hadlands. Graham Young was arrested at his father's house, and as he was led away, asked the police: 'Which ones are they doing me for, then?'

However, in custody Young claimed that he was innocent, despite the fact that a phial of Thallium was found in his jacket pocket, and a list of six names of Hadland's employees was found in his bedsitter. The list was significant: it included the two men who had died, and the four stricken with horrible illnesses. But Young could not resist for long his need to boast.

He detailed his first murder, that of his stepmother, and explained why he decided to poison his workmates. Graham Young said: 'I suppose I had ceased to see them as people – or, more correctly, a part of me had. They became guinea pigs.' Detective Chief Superintendent Harvey Young, in charge of the case, warned Graham that this confession could put him in jail for life. But the prisoner said: 'You have to prove that I did it.' He intended to withdraw his statement in court, which in due course he did.

On 3 December, Graham Young was charged with murdering Egle after the analysis of the ashes of his cremated corpse showed traces of Thallium in them. He pleaded Not Guilty. He was also charged with the murder of Fred Biggs and the attempted murders of two others and of further administering poison to two others.

In prison , Young enquired of his guards whether Madame Tussaud's waxworks in London were planning to put his effigy next to those of his heroes, Hitler and the poisoner, Palmer. He threatened to kill himself in the dock of the court if he were found Guilty. But there were no theatricals from the prisoner when he was convicted on all charges by a jury that took less than an hour to deliberate on the evidence.After a brief chat with his family, he was taken away to begin a life sentence in July 1972.

A DEADLY FUNGUS

Young was not sent back to Broadmoor but, initially, was sent to Wormwood Scrubs, then, to the top security Park Lane Mental Hospital near Liverpool. He was in this institution for two years before officials realised he had lost none of his madness. In 1990, they discovered that Graham had grown, in the prison grounds, a deadly fungus that he mixed with his own excrement to concoct a deadly toxin.

He was transferred to the top security prison of Parkhurst on the Isle of Wight where he was found dead in his cell on 2 August 1990. At first, officials thought that he had killed himself with one of his own poisons, but a post mortem revealed that a heart attack had been cause of death.

There were few people to weep for him, his sister, also called Winifred, felt sad for him. She said that he craved publicity and infamy, and he certainly achieved these ambitions. But she said that he was depressive and lonely. When she suggested he ease his loneliness by going to social clubs or dances, he replied; 'Nothing like that can help me, I'm afraid. You see, there is this terrible coldness inside of me...'